The Indispensable Teacher's Guide to Computer Skills

By Doug Johnson

PROFESSIONAL GROWTH SERIES®

A Publication of THE BOOK REPORT & LIBRARY TALK
Professional Growth Series

Linworth Publishing, Inc.
Worthington, Ohio

Library of Congress Cataloging-in-Publication Data

Johnson, Doug
      The Indispensable Teacher's Guide to Computer Skills/by Doug Johnson
            p. cm.–(Professional growth series)
      Includes biographical references (p.) and index.
      ISBN 0-938865-69-2
      1. School libraries–United States–Data processing.
      2. Instructional materials centers–United States–Data processing.
      3. Computer-assisted instruction–United States. 4. Media programs
(Education)–United States.   I. Title. II. Series.
      Z675.S3B773   1999
      027.8'0285–dc20

Published by Linworth Publishing, Inc.
480 East Wilson Bridge Road, Suite L
Worthington, Ohio 43085

Copyright©1999 by Linworth Publishing, Inc.

Series Information:
      From The Professional Growth Series

Table of Contents

Table of Contents continued

Introduction: A Work in Progress

 Those that know, do. Those that understand, teach.

–Aristotle

Word processing is usually the first, and often remains the primary, use of the computer by teachers. Teachers are writers—of worksheets, of study guides, of student comments, of curriculum guides, of letters to parents, of tests, of rubrics, of checklists, of announcements, of newsletters. You name it, we write it. Our schools operate primarily through the medium of verbal language, and those who are successful in school—as students, teachers or administrators—tend to be those who read, write, and speak well.

I have never lost my delight with the writing freedom the word processor has given me. I can remember from my first years of teaching the painful evenings I spent typing tests on mimeograph paper, of carefully removing the inverse waxy errors I'd made with a razor blade, and of quietly praying the faded blue print from previous years' worksheets would last for just one more run of 90 copies. My handwriting is illegible, so not typing student materials was never an option. (Plus I had to walk 10 miles to school—uphill both ways. But that's another story.)

My poor typing was, in fact, a disservice to my students. Each November, I'd pull that faded *Macbeth* test from my file cabinet and look through it. Spelling errors, missing words, and haphazard alignment of foils made the test harder than it needed to be for my students, and even worse were the questions that just didn't work because they were ambiguous or irrelevant. Each year, I would look at that test (all nine pages, 60-odd questions) and vow to type a revision of it. And each year, time would get short and I would use the old test, orally prefaced by an ever-lengthening set of corrections.

The word processor changed that. Finally, I could keep the questions that worked and only change the problematic ones. I could run a fresh mimeograph sheet through the dot matrix printer every year. And, oh happy days! I could check my words with a spell checker. Suddenly, I could eliminate the gross unfairness of the world's judging a writer's ideas by how those ideas were spelled. I was liberated, and I couldn't wait to start freeing up all the kids who suffered from the same problems I did.

Those same feelings of empowerment also hit me, in subsequent years, as I learned to use databases, spreadsheets, presentation programs, video editing, e-mail, the World Wide Web, and intranets. But word processing was my first true digital love.

This early experience with the word processor taught me a couple of things:

First, because of the digitization of information, *anything* can be a work in progress. Unlike my typed *Macbeth* test, teacher-produced materials can easily be modified and improved each time they are used. Spelling and grammar checkers can help clean up professional communication and student writing. Truly proficient computer users soon begin to take advantage of their word processor's desktop publishing features to add explanatory graphics, catchy fonts, and visual emphases. The homemade materials become indistinguishable from commercial materials—other than the flexibility to tailor-make them to the needs of an individual class.

> Teachers really do need to experience the power of technology on a personal level before they can successfully introduce it to students.

This work-in-progress phenomenon is growing. Curriculum can now be continuously revised. Guides and teacher-produced support materials can be published on the school's intranet and continuously updated. The latest student performance reports can be shared with parents, who can be given online access. Long-range plans can change as technologies, funding, or philosophies change. As the requests society makes on our curriculum grow and change, we can rapidly adapt.

The second thing I learned along with the word processor was that teachers need to experience the power of technology on a personal level before they can successfully introduce it to students. Spreadsheets are wonderfully involv-

ing, databases can be as intriguing to build as any model, and hypermedia shows can buck up the most reluctant speaker. But it takes an enthusiastic teacher to get kids away from the computer games and drills, and into these "knowledge construction sets." That won't happen unless teachers have taken the time and made the considerable effort to learn the software and use it to meet a genuine need of their own. Schools must provide opportunities for that to happen.

Teachers need technology first.

That's what this short book is about. It is my personal attempt at finding ways to empower teachers by describing practical technology skills they can and want to use, and want to share with their students. It's about using technology to make good things happen for both teachers and students. (I am not sure how we can ever do something that is good for one and not the other.)

This is not a stand-alone "how-to" manual for any specific technology skill, but rather an articulation, a framework, and a guide for teachers and teachers of teachers to help give them learning goals and suggestions about the resources they might use to meet those goals. I've also included some rather pragmatic reasons teachers need to work toward those goals. This book is a resource to be used along with relevant staff development opportunities, up-to-date hardware and software guides, and a nurturing human support system.

Oh, the word processor gave me one last insight. You can be a terrible writer, so long as you are a great reviser. Or should that read, *One* can be a terrible writer, but great reviser? Let's see...if I eliminate that, and move this...Anyway, here is the latest revision.

CHAPTER 1

Critical Components of Effective Staff Development

" *Imagine a school with children that can read or write, but with teachers who cannot, and you have a metaphor of the Information Age in which we live.* "

—Peter Cochrane

 WHY IT IS IMPERATIVE THAT TEACHERS BECOME COMPUTER LITERATE?

A computer will be a part of your future in one of two ways, I tell beginning users. One possibility is that it will be there to compensate for your lack of training and skills: the computer in the fast-food cash register will relieve you of the need to compute tax or make change. The computer will also relieve you of the higher pay that comes with a skilled job.

Another future might have you using the computer as a productivity tool to enhance your talents as a diagnostician in medicine or in mechanics; as a researcher in law or in academics; or as a communicator in business or engineering or art. The computer will then enhance your income as well.

If our schools are to produce graduates who can proficiently use the computer as a productivity tool, we first need teachers who are skilled at using technology to enhance their own abilities and are comfortable enough with these skills to fully integrate them into their classroom lessons.

Technology training for classroom teachers too often does little more than acquaint them with a few easy-to-open and -operate drill-and-practice pieces of software. These programs, like the small brain in the cash register, ask the student (or teacher) for little higher order thinking or creativity. Learning to use the computer as a productivity tool—for electronic research, for written communication, for assisted drawing or drafting, for database design, or for spreadsheet construction—requires more time for training and more equipment for practice than most districts have been willing to invest.

As educators, we must revisit our assumption that students always have first priority for technology. Schools need to take a step back to train teachers to use the technology as a productivity tool, before we will see the long-term gains in increased student skills.

Parents and administrators want computer-literate teachers. Students seek out teachers who meaningfully use technology. And teachers themselves acknowledge that computer skills are increasingly necessary and important in fulfilling their professional duties.

➤ WHY AREN'T MORE TEACHERS COMPUTER LITERATE?

Far too many teachers have fallen prey to the syndrome that Donald Norman, in his book *The Psychology of Everyday Things*, calls "learned helplessness." It's easy to acquire. Folks have learned to be helpless about a lot of things beside computers: music, cooking, languages, carpentry, writing, swimming. If we register a couple of negative experiences with an activity or skill, we quite easily rationalize our frustrations by saying, "I was just never very good at _____ (fill in the blank)."

Perhaps we need to put some of the responsibility for computer-illiterate teachers on our educational leaders. Rare are the districts that have stated visions of how technology is to be used and how its impact on the educational process is to be assessed. Even more rare are the districts that clearly articulate the specific skills they would like their teachers to have. "Computer literacy" as it applies to teachers can easily remain ill defined—a politically correct buzzword without meaning or purpose.

➤ SOME BASIC DO'S OF STAFF DEVELOPMENT IN TECHNOLOGY

It may be too late to save some teachers—the learned helplessness may be too deeply ingrained. But most are salvageable if your staff development program includes:

1 **ACCESS, ACCESS, ACCESS.** A computer in a teacher's room or office is probably the single best way to prevent learned helplessness. Teachers need to be able to check computers out to take home in the evenings, over the weekend, and especially during the summer. I have found that many teachers get tired of lugging computers back and forth and wind

For many years staff development for technology has gone something like this:

1 The teacher signs up for "Computer Basics" and completes the inservice training, leaving with a sense of mastery.

2 A week or two later, when the teacher gets a few minutes to use the building's computer, she sits down to find out that she remembers little of what she thought she had mastered. "Must need more training," she thinks.

3 Next time technology training rolls around, the teacher again signs up for "Computer Basics" and completes the training.

4 A week or two later, when the teacher gets a few minutes to use the building's computer, she sits down to find out that she remembers little of what she was taught. "Must need more training," she thinks.

5 Repeat steps 3 and 4 a couple more times.

6 The teacher finally decides that she just isn't adept with technology and begins to avoid computer inservice training at all cost.

up buying a computer for home within a year of beginning active computer use. Why have teachers not had more access to computers? Our best intentions and altruistic natures have led to us putting computers in our students' hands—through labs and classroom workstations—first. But often the result of those good intentions has been only superficial use of computers in schools, primarily with drill-and-practice software that never helps in improving higher order thinking skills or communication, and may not even be very good at teaching basic skills.

2 MEANINGFUL APPLICATION. I am not sure technology advocates have done anyone a favor by suggesting that computers make one's life easier. They may save a little time here and there, but the real benefit of computing is that it just plain makes one better at one's job. Our district staff development activities stress the use of the computer as a productivity tool *for the teacher.* We work hard to see that all teachers use word processing, e-mail, and a computerized record-keeping system in the form of an electronic grade book, spreadsheet or database. I am firmly convinced that teachers will not use productivity tools with kids until they themselves have experienced the empowering effect of technology on a personal basis. Oh, and teachers seem *not* to need instruction on how to use "drill-and-kill" applications.

3 TIME FOR PRACTICE. Learning to use a computer, it's said, requires about the same investment in time and energy as gaining rudimentary fluency in a second language. So how do you give a person more time? A savvy administrator who knows that a teacher is earnestly trying to master computer skills might temporarily release that individual from some supervisory responsibilities, understand if he or she doesn't sign up for building committees, look for others to do special assignments, or find ways to reduce the number of preps. Technology use should be accepted as a professional improvement goal. Inservice and workshop days for technology training are a must. A couple of laptop computers for teacher check-out can extend teachers' learning time from a couple of hours a day to literally any time they are not in class.

4 A TECHNOLOGY ENVIRONMENT. It's amazing what happens in a school when even a few teachers start using a computer. It gives everyone else in the building courage. The internal dialog goes something like, "Jeez, if Johnson can learn to use a computer—and I know I am a heck of a lot smarter than he is—so can I."

5 SUPPORT. We all need it, but some need it more than others. This can be formalized by holding follow-up sessions a few weeks after the initial training. But as important, it means having someone close to call. To this I would add, all persons providing instruction should remain as humane as possible. The teachers who teach technology skills

---

These are the steps we advise new computer users to follow when they hit a roadblock:

- Try again.
- Get a cup of coffee, go to the bathroom, stretch, and try again.
- Check the manual (optional).
- Call another teacher who was in the training.
- Ask your kids, the neighbors' kids, or a member of the local computer club.
- Call your media specialist.
- Call the computer coordinator.
- When all other avenues have been explored, call the district administrator in charge of technology. He or she can rarely help but is often a very sympathetic listener.

➤ SEVEN QUALITIES OF HIGHLY EFFECTIVE TECHNOLOGY TRAINERS

1 ABILITY TO SEE THAT THE PROBLEM IS ON THE DESK, NOT IN THE CHAIR. (RAY VANDER WIEL, AEA10, CEDAR RAPIDS, IOWA) When a problem arises, the best trainers assume it is a result of a hardware or software flaw — whether an actual bug or a design in the user interface that makes the technology confusing for normal people to use. It's sometimes tough to help people increase their knowledge without making them feel stupid or incompetent, but good teachers do. Comments like, "My third graders can do that," "You know, it works better when you plug it in," and, "No, the *other* right arrow," are *not* recommended.

2 SELF-CONTROL TO REFRAIN FROM MOUSE TOUCHING. Effective trainers are patient. One sure sign of this saintly virtue in teachers is that they never touch a student's mouse or keyboard. No matter how exasperating it becomes to watch that ill-coordinated teacher find and click on the correct button, an effective instructor's hands, white knuckled as they may be, stay well behind their backs.

3 ABILITY TO MAKE GREAT ANALOGIES. There is a theory that the only way we can think about a new thing is if we have some way to relate it to what we already know. Effective trainers can do that by creating analogies. "Your e-mail account is like a post office box. Your password is like your combination to get into it. Your e-mail address is like your mailing address—it tells the electronic postmaster where to send your e-mail." Now, here's the catch: Truly great analogists know when the comparisons break down, too. "Unlike a human postmaster, the electronic postmaster can't make intelligent guesses about an address. The extra dot, the *L* instead of a *1*, or a single juxtaposition of letters will keep your mail from being delivered."

4 CLEAR SUPPORT MATERIALS AND ADVANCED PLANNING. Few things are more comforting to teachers than being able to take home a cheat sheet that covers much of the same material that was taught in class. Until multistep tasks are repeated several times, most of us need reminders that are more descriptive than just notes taken in class. A short menu of task steps illustrated with screen shots is a gift for most technology learners.

Just as they take time to prepare good handouts, savvy technology teachers check out the lab or teaching area well in advance (a week is best) for potential problems with workstations, software versions, projection units, security systems, and network connections. Effective instructors leave little to chance.

5 KNOWING WHAT IS ESSENTIAL AND WHAT IS ONLY CONFUSING. An effective trainer will have a list of the skills learners should have mastered by the end of the training. As instruction proceeds, that list will be the basis for frequent checks for understanding. As an often-random thinker, I find such a list keeps me on track as an instructor and provides a class roadmap for the learner. Now, here's the catch with this one: truly great technology teachers know what beginning learners really need to know to make them productive and what might be conveyed that only serves to impress a captive audience with the technologist's superior intellect. ("The e-mail address comprises the username, the domain name, the subdomain name, the computer name, all referenced in a lookup table at the NIC." Like that.) It's an alpha wolf thing, especially common with males. Be aware of it, and strive as an instructor, instead, to use charm and a caring demeanor with the pack to achieve dominance.

6 ASSURANCE THAT IF IT BREAKS, WE'LL FIX IT. Kids catch on to technology with amazing rapidity for a very good reason: They aren't afraid to push buttons. They know if they mess something up, it's an adult's job to fix it. That's one nice thing about being a kid. However, we need to instill in most of our adult learners the courage to experiment. Rather than always answering direct questions about technology, effective trainers will often say, "Try it and see what happens. If you mess something up, I'll help you fix it." We tell our new technology learners that we can repair or replace anything but their original creations. The only real worry they should have is about backing up personal files.

7 PERSPECTIVE. Many of us who work with technology do so because we love it. We play with new software on the weekends, surf the Internet deep into the evening, and show off our new gadgets like other folks show off prize-winning zinnias, new powerboats, or successful children. I hesitate to use the term "abnormal," but we *are* in the minority. Most teachers see technology as a sometimes-helpful thing that should occupy about 1% of one's conscious thinking time. It's easy to lose the perspective that teachers are teachers first and technology users second—or third or fourth. Trainers who can remember what it was like before there were computers—the green grass, the singing birds, the books to read, the parties to attend, the fishing trips, the face-to-face human communication—tend to be more empathetic. Think back, think back. ...

have to be excellent teachers indeed. (See "Seven Qualities of Highly Effective Technology Trainers," opposite.)

6 A VARIETY OF TRAINING OPPORTUNITIES.
Adults don't all learn in the same way any more than kids do. Some people learn best in a class setting, step by step. Others like a rapid description of all the things a program can do, a written guide, and time to figure it out for themselves. (That's *my* personal learning style.) Some need one-on-one tutoring, some get by with the manual and a little privacy. Good instructional videotapes appeal to yet other teacher-learners. Training sessions before school, after school, and in the evenings all may work for some teachers. Classes need to be available both in the summer and during the school year. Good staff development programs will find a way to use different instructors with their own individual styles and teaching methods. While the needed skills are consistent from teacher to teacher, districts need to be sure a variety of methods and opportunities is available to individuals.

7 A LITTLE FEAR MONGERING. Let's face it. Computer illiterate teachers are not good for kids. It's time administrators and fellow teachers stop accepting excuses for other teachers' not having computer skills. But we educators may be too late. Kids, parents, businesses, and communities are already communicating that message very well.

▧ INFORMAL STAFF DEVELOPMENT

A word needs to be said about those among us who seem to pick up technology skills without ever attending a class. Strong self-motivation, a knack for technology, a built-in tutor in the form of a child or spouse all can provide individuals with the opportunity and incentive to learn independently of formal staff development efforts. These learners should be encouraged and should not be forced into classes for which they see no need. Skills identification and assessment, however, is still helpful to the independent learner. ("See Demonstration of Skills through Portfolio Assessment," below).

Informal staff development occurs in schools on a regular basis. A teacher who might be stuck on a particular application asks a fellow teacher or (increasingly) a student for help. A number of schools set up help desks, often staffed by high school students, for just such occurrences. Our schools' perceptive media specialists track individual requests for help and offer 20- to 30-minute after-school classes on a single topic or skill, like using e-mail attachments, importing a movie into a hypermedia stack, or creating a summary field in a database.

Routed newsletters and e-zines that offer tips about a particular application are useful to independent learners. The print periodical *ClarisWorks Journal* has proven popular, as has the electronic Dummies Daily basic computing tip **http://www.dummiesdaily.com**/, which is delivered via e-mail each day.

▧ MENTORING

Less formal than classes, but providing more structure than informal staff training, mentoring matches an experienced computer with a novice. We have experimented with a mentor program in our district, with somewhat mixed results in the final skill assessments.

By following these guidelines, a school can improve its chances for a successful mentoring program:

▶ Carefully select mentors. Make sure they have the skills they are supposed to be teaching. New technologies, new versions of software, or new instructional approaches may have been introduced in the district since the more experienced folks received their training.

Pick people who tend to keep current as independent learners.

▶ Ask for a log of hours spent in training. Teachers' days are more than full, and it's easy for most of us to put off tasks that aren't urgent. Requesting or requiring a log of mentor/mentee hours spent can help move the training up a teacher's priority list.

▶ Check to make sure participants remain compatible. On rare occasions, we have found that an assigned pair of teachers do not work well together. Don't wait until the end of the program to find this out. All teams should be visited several times a year, and if problems are discovered, teachers can be reteamed.

▶ Assess the progress of the participants. Use the same standards and assessment for a program that uses mentors for instructional delivery as you would for a program that uses classroom instruction or independent study

The Internet and e-mail have enhanced the opportunities for mentoring significantly. Quick responses to specific questions and less dependence on physical proximity are genuine benefits to "telementoring."

▷ CLASSES

Like many districts, ours offers a selection of classes throughout the school year, primarily in the evenings. Although voluntary, these classes still fill rapidly. Good technology training classes have the same characteristics as all good classes but are probably less forgiving of poor planning and teaching.

We have found the most learning occurs in staff development classes that:

▶ **ARE NOT MORE THAN THREE HOURS LONG.** Learning computer applications is intense work. In our experience, little is accomplished after two to three hours of direct

instruction. If an entire day is allocated for technology training, allow teachers to practice skills learned in the morning by applying them to personal projects in the afternoon.

▶ **HAVE A WELL-PREPARED, KNOWLEDGEABLE INSTRUCTOR.** See "Seven Qualities of Highly Effective Technology Trainers," above.

▶ **HAVE A TEACHING ASSISTANT FOR MORE THAN 5 TO 10 STUDENTS.** Most classes rapidly divide into those who can keep up and those who still can't work the mouse. A teaching assistant is a must for heterogeneous classes if all learners are to make progress. The assistant does not need to be a master teacher but does need to be familiar with the application being taught.

▶ **HAVE WELL-DEFINED OBJECTIVES.** If possible, include a brief list of major skills to be taught in the training session, so teachers can place themselves according to their skill levels. Calling a class "advanced" is not sufficiently descriptive.

▶ **INCLUDE GOOD SUPPORT MATERIALS.** Most participants want, and need, personal paper copies of the class's learning goals (agenda), recipe-type guides to software applications, and other resources, like Web page guides, sample documents, lesson plans, and templates. Handouts allow learners to focus on the instruction rather than the attempt to frantically write down every essential step of a complex task.

▶ **ARE TAUGHT IN A FUNCTIONING LAB.** Nothing takes the steam out of a technology workshop quicker than a poor physical environment. Insufficient workstations, a missing or unreadable projection device, poor network connections, a mix of software versions, and missing helper applications all can confuse the learners and impede teaching. Air-conditioning, few external disruptions and convenient break areas all contribute to a comfortable learning environment.

▶ SUGGEST IMMEDIATE SKILL APPLICATIONS.

I believe the best technology trainers are teachers who have actually used the technology in the classroom. These folks not only tell you *how* to use something but *why* you'd want to. They help teachers immediately use the software to create materials or lessons that will be used in their schools and classroom. With advanced notice, the participating teachers can be asked to bring personal working materials: class lists, lesson plans, or units.

▶ ARE OFFERED AT A VARIETY OF TIMES.

Coaching, club sponsorship, collaboration meetings, and just drop-dead tiredness all keep teachers away from classes at certain times. A major factor in successful classes is learners who are rested and alert whether they are preschoolers or "postschoolers."

▷ TRAINING ON DEMAND AND IN-CLASSROOM TRAINING

Increasingly, we are offering what we call TOD: Training on Demand. Our computer coordinator offers the staff customized training, provided the following conditions are met:

- Five or more teachers, secretaries, administrators, or other staff members all want the same training.

- These folks have a clear idea of what it is they want to learn.

- They agree on a common training time of not less than two hours.

- They reserve a lab for the training time.

A natural offshoot of TOD has the computer coordinator or media specialist working

> Many teachers have discovered that, along with teaching summer school, painting houses, and working at Kmart, they can use summer for critical professional development.

with the classroom teacher along with his or her class. Although labor intensive, this is probably the best means of assuring technology is immediately integrated effectively into the curriculum. If teachers have multiple classes all working on the same project, such an arrangement can be a powerful learning experience for the students as well. During the first one or two classes, the teacher learns the skills along with the students. By the third class period, the classroom teacher is helping individual students. And by the end of the day, the teacher is feeling comfortable enough to teach the skills and should not need the support of the staff developer the next time the skills are taught. This kind of program works well provided teachers stay with their classes and understand that they are responsible for teaching the skill alone in subsequent years, when the computer coordinator or media specialist will be working with other teachers.

▷ SUMMER ACADEMIES

The old joke was that the three best reasons for being a teacher were June, July, and August. Now many teachers have discovered that along with teaching summer school, painting houses, and working at Kmart, they can use summer for critical professional development. Many districts use the larger blocks of time to offer summer technology training opportunities that run from a few days to a week or longer.

Organization of these academies varies according to district need. For schools with a large number of beginning teachers, it works well to have a prescribed course of study that all participants follow. For districts that have a wide range of teacher competencies or needs, a smorgasbord of full- or half-day classes can be successful.

Characteristics of good summer academies include:

▶ **OUT-OF-SCHOOL SETTING.**
Advantageous as it is to teach intensive technology training at a time when there's no pressure to prepare for classes, some districts move the training out of the school setting. College campuses, summer camps, and resorts all offer different venues that promote a special, more relaxed atmosphere.

▶ **EVALUATION.** Both teachers and learners need to help the summer academy improve by indicating where classes are strong and how they could be improved. We give the instructors evaluation forms to refer to as they prepare for the class. (See evaluation in the Appendix).

▶ **RELIABLE, WELL-PAID INSTRUCTORS.**
High-quality instruction, more than any other factor, will determine whether teachers continue to take classes at your district's academy. We pay our instructors $50 per hour ($300 per day, or $1,500 per week). This usually creates a pool of trainers from which to choose, and we only rehire trainers who get very high marks on class evaluations.

▶ **HELPFUL INFORMATIONAL MATERIALS.**
The informational brochures and registration forms should include detailed descriptions of classes being offered, including a summary of skills being taught (again, to help participants place themselves in developmentally appropriate classes). Cost information, maps to and of the training location, and registration deadlines are helpful to the participant. (A sample is provided in the Appendix.) Easy-to-read signs that point to teaching and commons areas is always appreciated.

▶ **WELL-STOCKED LABS WITH RELIABLE EQUIPMENT.** The investment in time and, often,

money by the participant makes the need for good facilities paramount. If the academy is held outside the district, the coordinator of the program needs to personally check facilities and equipment to make sure they meet the academy's needs. Labs with fast, memory-laden computers and good network connections are a plus, as is having one or two more computers than students, in case a computer malfunctions. (I've only *heard* of this happening.) Lots of competent, on-site tech help is also a must.

▶ **FOOD, T-SHIRTS, NOTEBOOKS, DOOR PRIZES, ANNOUNCEMENTS.** The very best academies create a special atmosphere of camraderie and human networking. Common meeting and eating areas and special whole-group welcomes bring participants together. The friendly atmosphere can be developed by making sure registration fees are sufficient to give participants plenty of food, notebooks, computer disks, T-shirts, and other "freebies." These items often can be provided or their costs subsidized by technology vendors or other academy sponsors. The educational climate is as important for adult learners as it is for children.

▶ RECOMMENDED EQUIPMENT AND SOFTWARE FOR STAFF DEVELOPMENT EFFORTS

The skills suggested in this book can be taught using a variety of software titles running on either Wintel (PC) or Macintosh computers. Computers that are reasonably fast, have adequate memory and storage capacities, and can be networked make the greatest range of instruction possible. For teachers who work in multiple buildings or wish to work at home, the expense of laptop computers can be justified. CD-ROM drives, video-in/video-out ports, and sound cards are all desirable features for teachers wishing to do multimedia projects with students.

My theory about software is that, often, less is more. Districts should adopt a standard set of software around which all training can be developed. All software titles should be available for both Macintosh and Wintel computers, so students and teachers can interchange files from machines throughout the school and at home regardless of platform. Look for product licenses that allow a single copy of the program to be used on both a teacher's school and home computers.

I am not endorsing any of the brand-name software listed below. Many fine products can be substituted for these titles, I'm sure, but these products have worked well for us.

All teachers need:

▶ AN INTEGRATED PRODUCTIVITY PACKAGE.

ClarisWorks and Microsoft-Works can be used by both teachers and students. For teachers who might want more sophisticated features, office packages such as Microsoft Office are available at bargain basement educational prices. But be aware that the more sophisticated the software program, the more demanding its hardware requirements, and that additional features usually mean more complexity and a steeper, longer learning curve.

▶ TELECOMMUNICATIONS SOFTWARE.
The most recent Web browsers make providing the needed tools fairly simple. Both Netscape and Microsoft Explorer allow the user to read Web pages, use newsgroups, find gopher sites and FTP remote files, and send and receive e-mail. In our district, we have chosen to use Eudora Light, a free dedicated e-mail program, so students and teachers can use a single computer to access their e-mail without having to recon-

> **All software titles should be available for both Macintosh and Wintel computers, so students and teachers can interchange files from machines throughout the school and at home regardless of platform.**

figure the e-mail program each time or worry about storing their messages. (Both configuration files and storage folders are kept on floppy diskette.) Teachers will eventually need helper applications such as a file decompression program, Adobe Acrobat Reader, a GIF converter, and a virus checker. Most of these are inexpensive shareware or freeware.

▶ MULTIMEDIA/HYPERMEDIA SOFTWARE.
Depending on curricular needs, a variety of software programs help teachers put together multimedia or hypermedia presentations. Many teachers find the Slideshow feature in the ClarisWorks word processor meets their needs. PowerPoint is growing in popularity. We teach HyperStudio to teachers who like to work with students on multimedia presentations. For those who want to do Web-based publications or multimedia, Claris Homepage is a simple-to-use alternative to having to learn complex HTML coding.

▶ TEACHER TOOLS.
Simple graphics programs like The PrintShop, collections of clip art, and crossword puzzle and word search creators are useful, though not essential.

▶ DATABASES.
With the proliferation of shared networked databases, we are finding that the relatively simple programs that come in integrated packages are not powerful enough. FileMaker Pro, which is easily networked and works cross-platform, has been useful to our teachers.

▶ GRADEBOOKS.
Teachers need record-keeping tools such as commercially produced grade books, individual education plan templates, and electronic portfolio organizers. These may be stand-alone products, part of a

larger student management system, or individually developed by teachers. Our district has successfully used MicroGrade for electronic grade bookkeeping.

▶ PUTTING THE PIECES TOGETHER
The CODE 77 Program: A Formal Staff Development Plan that Worked

In 1992, a team of five teachers and the district media supervisor decided that Mankato Public Schools needed a formal plan for improving the computer literacy of our 400 teachers. On that group's recommendation, the district media supervisor requested and received capital funds from the administrative council and school board for 40 computers, printers, modems, carrying bags, and software packages. This gave individual computers to approximately 10% of our full-time teachers. The program was named CODE 77—Computers On Desks Everywhere in District 77. The project has been funded for each year since at varying levels.

The CODE 77 project has the following characteristics that make it unlike many other staff development efforts in technology:

▶ The project is long term and far-reaching, and eventually will give all teachers in the district computer access.

▶ Computers are awarded on the basis of a competitive grant proposal. Participants have ideas about what they will do with the equipment before receiving it.

▶ Computers are assigned to individuals, not buildings, grade levels, or departments. The teachers keep the computers as long as they are with the district.

▶ Thirty hours of inservice training for teachers is required. All training is done outside regular school hours, with no extra pay for the participants.

▶ Participants have the option of getting graduate credit through a local university for taking the class.

▶ All participants complete assessments of their learning through rubrics and present portfolios to the school board.

▶ The current year's CODE 77 participants recommend modifications to the program for the subsequent year.

▶ The current year's participants serve as informal mentors to the subsequent year's participants.

Funds are appropriated in April, and one-page proposal forms are sent to all teachers in the district. (See sample application form in the Appendix.) Teams consisting of the district media supervisor, computer coordinator, and building principal choose the participants on the following criteria:

▶ uniqueness of proposal

▶ likelihood of goal achievement

▶ wide representation of grade levels and subject areas throughout the district

Proposals are received and participants selected in May. Participants receive their "bundles" on the first day of a three-day training session during the summer. Seven weekly evening classes continue through the fall. Participants receive hands-on training in general computer use, file management, word processing, student record-keeping, multimedia production, and use of spreadsheets, databases, graphics, and the Internet.

A board report is given in March. This report in the past has included written evaluations of the program, shared portfolios of computer-generated materials, videotape presentations, and formal verbal reports by teacher participants and the media supervisor.

As their computers need replacement, teachers who have completed the basic program may apply for updated computers. The new computers come with 15 hours of advanced computer training in database use, Web page creation, or multimedia production. (Early CODE 77 participants were not taught Internet skills because the Internet was not available in the district at the time. This second-phase training helps earlier participants catch up.)

⟩ DEMONSTRATION OF SKILLS THROUGH PORTFOLIO ASSESSMENT

As time goes by, districts find that some teachers have acquired basic computer literacy skills outside formal staff development programs. To ask these teachers to complete many hours of formal training seems counterproductive. However, schools still need a way to determine if those teachers have at least minimal computer literacy skills. One way of doing that is by asking teachers, in lieu of taking the formal computer training classes, to create portfolios that demonstrate their computer skills.

A portfolio must allow the teacher to demonstrate the same skills as those taught in the computer classes. Specific guidelines for completing the portfolio follow:

▶ At the time he or she applies for the program, the teacher must indicate to both the district computer coordinator and the building principal the choice to complete a portfolio instead of taking the CODE 77 classes.

▶ Each section of the portfolio needs to be turned in to the computer coordinator at least one week prior to the class that teaches the corresponding skills. (Sections may be turned in earlier or all at one time, but before the classroom training.)

▶ A teacher may take the class on an individual skill and turn in the corresponding section of the portfolio after the class.

▶ All sections must be completed in a way that meets the quality standards listed.

▶ The portfolio must be in a three-ring notebook, well organized, with tabs and a table of contents. All pages must be three-hole punched and clearly labeled, and must include the date of creation and the creator's name. Handouts of the skill rubrics serve as an introduction to the portfolio.

⟩ COMPUTER SKILL RUBRICS

Five years ago, when Mankato Area Public Schools began its formal staff development program to train teachers how to use technology, I wrote a series of rubrics (graduated performance indicators) that described what the district expected a teacher to be able to do after 30 hours of formal computer instruction and six to nine months of practice.

Since that time, new technologies (primarily the Internet) have come into the schools and many teachers have rapidly mastered the basics. Consequently, I have written two additional sets of rubrics: "Internet Skills for Teachers" and "Advanced CODE 77 Rubrics."

There is some overlap among the rubric sets. For example, the basic rubrics contain two Internet skills that also are in the "Internet Skills for Teachers" rubrics. Assessment of student skills is addressed in both the basic and advanced rubrics, but at different levels of complexity. Each set of rubrics should be able to stand by itself if it is to be used as the outline for a series of classes or staff development workshops or as part of a college course; therefore, some duplication is unavoidable.

Each of the next three chapters lists a set of these rubrics and describes them in more detail. A subsequent chapter describes how to use the rubrics to help evaluate staff development efforts.

CHAPTER 2

Basic CODE 77 Skills

Computers are like Old Testament gods:
lots of rules and no mercy.
—Joseph Campbell

➤ USING THE BASIC CODE 77 RUBRICS

The Basic CODE 77 rubrics primarily address professional productivity. They are the foundation on which more complex technology and technology-related professional skills are built. Teachers who have mastered these skills are able to use the computer to improve their traditional instructional tasks such as writing, record-keeping, designing student materials, and presenting lessons. These skills also build the confidence teachers need to use technology to restructure the educational process.

Each of the 10 rubrics has four levels:

> **LEVEL 1:** Pre-awareness
> **LEVEL 2:** Awareness
> **LEVEL 3:** Mastery
> **LEVEL 4:** Advanced

Prior to training, we assume most teachers are at level 1 or 2, and our training efforts are designed with that assumption. By the end of the training, we anticipate teachers will be at level 3 or 4 in most skill areas and will have gone up at least one level in all areas.

These rubrics then serve two purposes: By asking teachers to complete an anonymous self-assessment, using the rubrics before training and again after training, we can judge the effectiveness of our staff development efforts. Simple graphs showing the percentage of training participants at each level pre- and post-training are constructed. (See chapter five, "Assessing Staff Development.") These results may be shared with staff development committees and administration.

The rubrics also serve to provide a road map for teachers wanting to improve their computer skills. By examining the specific skills described, teachers know in which areas they need to continue to take classes or practice.

I have placed the rubrics in the order I would teach the skills. For example, I like to communicate with my students via e-mail, so I placed networking skills early in the program. Teachers seem to quickly understand the advantages of word processing and the use of electronic grade books, so I teach word processing early, too. I know that I will be using the concepts of graphic handles, alignment, and resizing when constructing database layouts, so I teach those skills in an early graphics class. The more complex and specialized the skill, the later I put it. I teach the issues surrounding ethical computer use in nearly every class.

Below are the instructions to teachers for completing a self-assessment and the rubrics themselves. Following each rubric is:

▶ a checklist of specific objectives a three- to four-hour training session can meet for most new computer users (two rubrics require two sessions, each with its own set of objectives); in some areas, I have also suggested advanced skills

▶ items a teacher portfolio might include that would demonstrate competency in this area.

▶ a short explanation of the uses to which a teacher might put this skill, and some student applications (or implications) of the skill.

▶ when appropriate, FREE ADVICE about teaching the skill.

> The rubrics also serve to provide a road map for teachers wanting to improve their computer skills.

Please feel free to use and modify the rubrics for your district's specific needs, and as technology changes.

By the way, these rubrics can also be modified to help benchmark student performance. See Jamison McKenzie's adaptation of these rubrics for that purpose at **<http://wwwbhs1. bham.wednet.edu/>**.

▶ TEACHER INSTRUCTIONS FOR USING THE CODE 77 BASIC RUBRICS

This is an anonymous assessment. You do not need to sign the pre- or post-test tool. Individual results wil be aggregated to determine how effective the program has been for the group as a whole. You should, however, keep track of your own individual progress.

Please judge your level of achievement in each of the following competencies. Circle the number that best reflects your current level of skill attainment. (Be honest, but be kind.) At the end of the training program, you will complete the same set of rubrics to reflect your level of skill attainment at that time. (Level 3 is considered mastery.) This tool is to help measure the effectiveness of our training program and to help you do a self-analysis to determine the areas in which you should continue to learn and practice. Keep a copy of these rubrics to refer to during the training.

I Basic computer operation

SELF-ASSESSMENT

LEVEL 1   I do not use a computer.

LEVEL 2   I can use the computer to run a few specific, preloaded programs. It has little effect on either my work or home life. I am somewhat anxious I might damage the machine or its programs.

LEVEL 3   I can set up my computer and peripheral devices, load software, print, and use most of the operating system tools like the scrapbook, clock, note pad, find command, and trash can (recycling bin). I can format a data disk.

LEVEL 4   I can run two programs simultaneously and have several windows open at the same time. I can customize the look and sounds of my computer. I use techniques like shift-clicking to work with multiple files. I look for programs and techniques to maximize my operating system. I feel confident enough to teach others some basic operations.

CLASS OBJECTIVES: INSTALLATION (2 HOURS)

1 Sign for your computer. Complete serial number and inventory report. Complete the pretraining rubric assessment.

2 Unpack your computer and printer, and check to make sure they work.

3 Install software:
- Word processor, database, spreadsheet, clipart
- Grade book program and other teacher utilities
- Web browser and e-mail program
- Printer software
- Virus program
- Image capture software

4 Register software

5 Set time, date, background, and volume in computer control panels.

6 Learn how to use and care for your CD-ROM drive.

7 Know computer care basics about:
- dampness
- dust
- drops
- magnetism
- power surges
- excess worry—it's not wise

YOUR PORTFOLIO MUST INCLUDE:

1. a page listing your computer's make, model number, serial number, amount of RAM, and size of hard drive

2. a list of software on the computer that you have installed

3. a formatted data disk

4. a brief written description of how to:
   - change the computer's time and date
   - find a file using the find command
   - remove an unwanted file from your computer

5. a test printout from your printer

BASIC COMPUTER OPERATIONS (1 HOUR)

8 Use the mouse effectively and know the terms:
- point
- click and double-click/left and right mouse buttons
- pull-down menu
- drag
- select, resize, and move windows
- scroll bars
- trash can/recycling bin

9 Know the difference between commercial software, freeware, and shareware. Know copyright issues surrounding computer software use, and the significance of those issues in an educational setting.

10 Use the Finder/Taskbar menu to determine which programs are running and use the Special/Start menu to shut down the computer.

11 Understand some ergonomic factors that can help prevent eyestrain and wrist stress.

 HOMEWORK: Practice your mouse skills by playing at least 20 games of solitaire.

> Fear of accidentally damaging the physical machine or destroying programs or files through inadvertent keystrokes can retard the exploration necessary to the learning process.

➤ TEACHER NEED FOR BASIC COMPUTER OPERATION SKILLS

This set of skills may seem so self-evident that it does not require elaboration, but many teachers' fears can be eased with instruction in basic computer operation. Fear of accidentally damaging the physical machine or destroying programs or files through inadvertent keystrokes can retard the exploration necessary to the learning process.

On a pragmatic level, teachers who can set up their own computers are more likely to move them where they will be convenient to work with. A teacher who can install or reinstall programs does not need to wait for a technician. The ability to do simple trouble-shooting for loose cables, a working electrical outlet, or even a switched-on monitor lowers the frustration of both the teacher and the computer professional.

➤ STUDENT NEED FOR BASIC COMPUTER OPERATION SKILLS

While it seems some students are born with a mouse in their hands and come to school with better mouse skills than many of us adults will ever have, they still need instruction on proper use of computers, keyboarding skills, and proper techniques for starting and shutting down the computer. Students need to understand classroom and lab rules and policies: May a student use a program from home? A disk from home? Where do students store their work—on the computer, on a floppy disk, or on the network? What programs are for student use and when? Is there a desktop security program running?

|| File Management

SELF-ASSESSMENT

LEVEL 1 I do not save any documents I create using the computer.

LEVEL 2 I save documents I've created but I cannot choose where they are saved. I do not back up my files.

LEVEL 3 I have a filing system for organizing my files and can locate files quickly and reliably. I back up my files to a floppy disk or other storage device on a regular basis.

LEVEL 4 I regularly run a disk optimizer on my hard drive and use a backup program to make copies of my files on a weekly basis. I have a system for archiving files I do not need on a regular basis, to conserve my computer's hard drive space.

CLASS OBJECTIVES:
FILE MANAGEMENT (3 HOURS)

1 Identify the two magnetic storage devices that come with your computer, format a 3.5 inch disk, and understand how to create backup copies of programs and why it is important to do so.

2 Understand the difference between applications, data files, and utility programs.

3 Create a folder system to organize your hard drive.

4 Open a new word processing file, save it to a folder, close the file, and quit the application.

5 Find, open, and save documents from within an application.

6 Use the Find program to locate lost files.

7 Connect to the building network to locate shared folders and/or personal archive space for files.

YOUR PORTFOLIO MUST INCLUDE:

1. a diagram of how you have your files and programs organized on your hard drive

2. a formatted data disk with a copied file that would serve as a back up

3. a brief written description of how you plan to back-up your personally created files

FREE ADVICE: *Teach beginning computer users to save all their documents to the desktop. They can later be moved to a folder after the application is closed. This rapidly familiarizes them with the filing system of the computer.*

Advise teachers to save all original documents in subfolders in a single FILES folder. That way only a single folder needs to be copied to create a backup and no files will be missed.

File names should be as descriptive as possible. A file called: "Unit 1 study guide 3-97" is far more easily found than one just called "Study guide."

TEACHER NEED FOR BASIC FILE MANAGEMENT SKILLS

The ability to easily create, store, and locate programs and files on a computer or network makes a teacher efficient and confident. Teachers experience huge time savings when a document needs to be created only once and then can be modified each time it is reused. For that to happen, teachers need to be able to create a sustainable organizing system so the materials they create can readily be found.

Teachers can save time by creating multiple versions of commonly used materials. Reusable models for letters to a parent, lesson plans, or unit reviews can be made by using the SAVE AS command and renaming the original file or by using an application's template creation feature.

HOMEWORK: Locate and open the word processing file you created in class. Modify it and save it under a new name on a folder both on your hard drive and on a floppy disk.

Teachers also find it advantageous to keep easily found copies of communications sent to fellow staff members, students, and parents. Remember the old saw: A memorandum serves not to inform the reader but to protect the writer.

STUDENT BENEFITS

Students will be the recipients of teaching materials that are clear, professional, and current because they are easily modified.

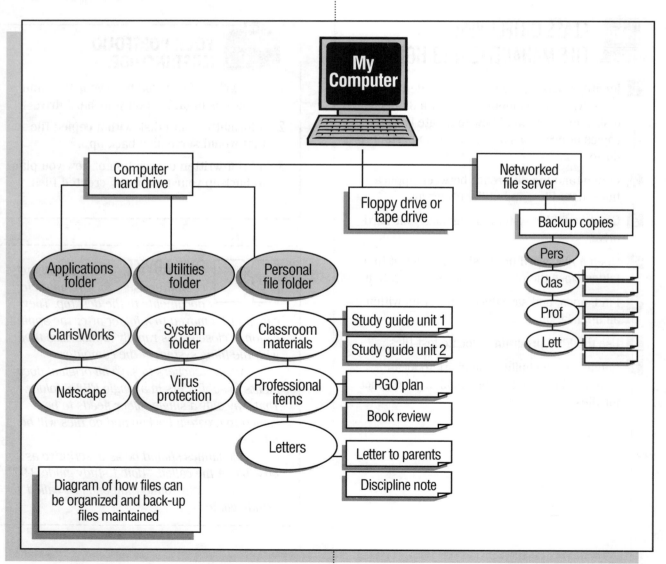

Diagram of how files can be organized and back-up files maintained

III Word Processing

CLASS OBJECTIVES: WORD PROCESSING FUNDAMENTALS (3 HOURS)

1 Understand the uses of word processing in an educational setting. Understand differences among word processors. Know the major differences between how one uses a typewriter and a word processor.

2 Open a new word processing file.

3 Set Preferences/Options to show special formatting characters such as spaces, carriage returns, and tabs.

4 Type in text and delete text by letter, word, sentence, and document.

5 Insert text at the beginning, middle, and end of a document.

6 Cut and paste text. Copy and paste text.

7 Use SELECT ALL and UNDO commands.

8 Edit text by changing font, size, and style. Know how to change style to plain text. Know when to use serif and sans serif fonts.

9 Know how to create columns using tabs.

10 Change paragraph justification and line spacing. Change the margins for a document.

11 Use the spell checker and thesaurus.

12 Create a footer that includes an automatic page number.

13 View an entire document and print the document.

14 Save a document under another name. Save the document to a specific folder.

15 Switch between multiple documents on a desktop, and be able to view multiple documents at the same time.

YOUR PORTFOLIO MUST INCLUDE BOTH THE PRINTOUT AND FILE OF A SAMPLE WORKSHEET OR PARENT COMMUNICATION THAT DEMONSTRATES:

1. half-inch margins with at least one paragraph inset to 1-inch margins

2. two text sizes, two fonts, underlined text, italicized text, and bold text

3. text that is left justified, center justified, and right justified

4. four rows of text in at least three aligned columns

5. a circled word that was flagged by the spell checker and a word replaced using the thesaurus

6. an automated page number in either a footer or header

▶ TEACHERS' USES OF THE WORD PROCESSOR

Word processing consistently ranks as the most used computer tool for teachers. Teachers can use the tool to:

- ▶ create instructional materials
  - ■ worksheets and study guides
  - ■ overhead transparencies
  - ■ original stories and essays
  - ■ create tests, checklists, and rubrics
  - ■ communicate with
    - ■ students
    - ■ parents (newsletters)
    - ■ other teachers
    - ■ administrators
    - ■ the community
- ▶ keep student records, learning plans, and assessments
- ▶ write grants, curricula, and class assignments

Nothing new here. Writing has always been a big part of a teacher's job. What has changed is that these materials are now:

- ▶ easily modified
- ▶ easily stored and located
- ▶ easily checked for grammar and spelling errors
- ▶ easily read by all readers (not all handwriting is)
- ▶ easily supplemented with helpful graphics and formatting
- ▶ professional in appearance
- ▶ easily shared among staff members (via disk, shared network folders, Web site, or e-mail attachment)

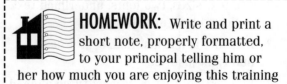

HOMEWORK: Write and print a short note, properly formatted, to your principal telling him or her how much you are enjoying this training

▶ STUDENT USES OF THE WORD PROCESSOR

Students can, and should, use the word processor for nearly all their written work. Process writing is greatly enhanced when the writer knows that early versions of one's work are simple to change. Some pragmatic cautions:

- ▶ Students need to be taught to back up files of original work.
- ▶ Students need instruction about the limitations of spelling and grammar checkers.
- ▶ Schools should adopt only cross-platform word processing. Students can then work on their files at home, regardless of the type of computer their family owns.
- ▶ Teachers need to determine how time at the computer is best spent: brainstorming, composing, editing, or formatting. For most schools, student access time is limited.

ADVANCED WORD PROCESSING SKILLS

1. Use shift-click to open multiple documents or chose multiple items.
2. Use Find-Replace command.
3. Create bullets and special characters.
4. Create multiple views of a single document.
5. Create hanging indents.
6. Set custom tabs.
7. Copy paragraph formats.
8. Use keyboard short cuts.
9. Create columns in a document
10. Force a page break
11. Create sections in a document.
12. Add fonts to your system.
13. Place and resize a graphic. Use text wrap.
14. Create tables

IV Network Use

CLASS OBJECTIVES: E-MAIL (3 HOURS)

1 Understand how the school is networked and how to obtain an e-mail account.

2 Know your e-mail user name and password.

3 Open the e-mail program.

4 Check and configure settings—understand username, e-mail address, and password.

5 Get new mail.

6 Read and delete a message.

7 Send a message.

8 Reply to a message, forward a message, and print a message.

9 Create a nickname file.

10 Set up a nickname for a group with multiple e-mail addresses.

11 Create a signature file.

12 Organize and store sent and received messages.

13 Understand "netiquette" as it applies to e-mail use.

YOUR PORTFOLIO MUST INCLUDE:

1. the printout of an e-mail you have sent and an e-mail you have received

2. a printout of your signature file

3. the printed results of an online ERIC or computer catalog search

4. the printout of a Web page on a topic of educational interest

5. the printout of the findings of an Internet search of an education topic using Yahoo, Lycos, Excite, or a similar tool

ADVANCED E-MAIL SKILLS

1. send, receive, and open attachments

2. subscribe, unsubscribe, and send a message to an electronic mailing list

3. use search tools to located e-mail address

4. find sources of student projects that use e-mail

➤ TEACHER NEED FOR BASIC E-MAIL SKILLS

As educators become more comfortable with e-mail, a pattern of growth emerges:

1 PERSONAL USE. Many teachers begin using e-mail because they have a child (often in college), friend, or professional colleague who has an e-mail account. The personal nature of the correspondence makes using the computer compelling enough to begin mastering its basic operation.

2 CONDUCTING SCHOOL BUSINESS. Using e-mail for certain tasks is becoming a standard operating procedure in schools where the resources are adequate. Once all teachers have networked computers on their desks, the school bulletin, departmental information, class attendance reporting, team-planning, and parent communications can all be effectively done electronically

 **FREE ADVICE:** *E-mail is often one of the first applications that reluctant teachers want to use. These beginning users more than most need recipe type instruction lists and hands-on classes. And not just on using the email program, but also about general computer operations like opening applications and files, text-editing, mousing, and even keyboarding. You may need to budget LOTS of time for "e-mail" instruction.*

One of the skills users seem most grateful for being taught is how to determine if a bounced message is caused by a faulty address or by network problems.

Lessons in online etiquette (netiquette) need to taught at the same time as the network skills themselves.

 HOMEWORK: Send at least three e-mail messages to associates and print out their responses.

Subscribe to the *Word of the Day* newsletter:

To subscribe send an e-mail to **word-of-the-day@parlez.net** with "subscribe" as the subject (please make sure your return address is correctly configured in your browser!) Or simply fill out the subscription form at **http://www.parlez.com/word-of-the-day/**.

Subscriptions are free.

3 OBTAINING INFORMATION. Educators soon find there is a wealth of information that can be obtained using their e-mail accounts. Discussion lists, electronic magazines and journals, and daily quotes, jokes, and vocabulary words can keep the reader current on almost any topic.

4 CREATING CLASSROOM ACTIVITIES. As many classroom teachers get excited about how e-mail has provided them with new learning opportunities, they will be anxious to get their students using this resource productively. Judi Harris' wonderful book *Way of the Ferret* (ISTE, 2nd ed., 1995) and Al Rogers' exciting Global Schoolhouse Network Web site **<http://www.gsn.org/>** and its HILITES mailing list are invaluable sources about these kinds of projects.

CLASS OBJECTIVES: ACCESSING INFORMATION ON THE INTERNET (3 HOURS)

1 Understand the unique properties of the World Wide Web.

2 Know what a Web browser does and the brand names of at least two popular browsers.

3 Configure the browser to a home page and configure e-mail settings.

4 Show location bar.

5 Use page links to navigate.

6 Know the functions of the tool bar items on Netscape.

7 Use forward and back buttons to navigate.

8 Directly enter a URL for a location.

9 Use Yahoo to locate information on a topic.

10 Use a search engine to locate information on a topic.

11 Print a page from the World Wide Web.

12 Create and arrange bookmarks.

13 Know and understand the district's acceptable use policy for Internet use

FREE ADVICE: *An understanding of copyright issues around the World Wide Web and other Internet resources should be taught when these skills are taught. Carol Simpson's Copyright for Schools (Linworth, 2nd ed. 1997) is an understandable guide to these complex issues.*

 HOMEWORK: Find 10 Web sites on a single topic of interest to you or on an area of your curriculum. Create bookmarks to them.

ADVANCED: (see also Chapter 3 of this book)

1. Understand the process for creating an original HTML page.

2. Know what the following "helper" applications do:
   - Telnet
   - GIFConverter
   - Abode Acrobat Reader
   - Sound Machine
   - QuickTime
   - Stuffit and UnZip

3. Use selection criteria to determine the reliability of information taken from Internet resources.

➤ TEACHER NEED FOR BASIC WORLD WIDE WEB USE SKILLS

Graphic browsers like Netscape and Explorer have done for the Internet what the Macintosh and Windows interfaces did for operating systems: take complex and confusing tasks and make them simple enough for everyone to use. That is a good thing since storing information in digital formats and accessing it using a network is increasingly becoming the standard way of doing business.

The World Wide Web, of course, is a tremendous source of professional information:

▶ lesson plans, activities, and support materials

▶ links to online projects

▶ professional research

▶ educational journals and magazines

▶ state and local educational data

▶ news

Lots of books about teacher, student, and parent Internet resources are being published.

Teachers can create bookmark "bibliographies" of curricular sources for their students. These can be either bookmark files or Web pages that include the addresses as links. Preselecting sites helps students get into the material faster. An extension of using Internet resources as classroom support materials involves moving the class itself on to the Web. High schools and colleges that are willing to become "virtual institutions" are now offering online classes and coursework.

As well as obtaining information from the Internet, teachers can use the Web as a practical and effective means to provide information about their classes and programs. Just as the school district's Web server can help students, parents, and the public easily access current activity schedules, staff directories, lunch menus, and policies, teacher-created Web pages can help students access class assignments and handouts.

The Web can also be an exciting way for students to share their work with a wide audience. Creative writing and art, results of student research, and the products of other classroom activities can be displayed on a district's Web server for other students throughout the world to examine and react to. Students in teacher preparation programs have ready access to student work for practice evaluating.

Many students are finding the Internet to be a primary source of information. And nowhere is it more obvious that the teacher's role in the educational process is moving from being the "sage on the stage" to the "guide by the side" than when students start using Internet resources to fulfill classroom assignments. Teacher questioning moves from simple recall questions about curricular topics to queries such as:

▶ "How did you find your information?"

▶ "Is it relevant to the problem you are trying to solve?"

▶ "Is the information reliable, accurate, and up-to-date?"

▶ "What are the implications of this information to you, the community, or the nation?"

▶ "How can you use this information and how can you effectively communicate it to others?"

Redefined teaching role? You bet. Just as or more important? You bet.

> **Teachers can use the Web as a practical and effective means to provide information about their classes and programs.**

V Graphics Use

SELF-ASSESSMENT

LEVEL 1   I do not use graphics in my word processing or presentations, nor can I identify any uses or features they might have that would benefit the way I work.

LEVEL 2   I can open and create simple pictures with the painting and drawing programs. I can use programs like PrintShop.

LEVEL 3   I use both premade clip art and simple original graphics in my word processed documents and presentations. I can edit clip art, change its size, and place it on a page. I can purposefully use most of the drawing tools and can group, ungroup, and align objects. I can use the clipboard to take graphics from one application for use in another. The use of graphics in my work helps clarify or amplify my message.

LEVEL 4   I use graphics not only for my work but with students to help them improve their own communications. I can use graphics and the word processor to create a professional-looking newsletter.

CLASS OBJECTIVES: PLACING GRAPHICS IN DOCUMENTS (3 HOURS)

1 Locate the graphics tools menu in a word processor.

2 Import a graphic from the Scrapbook/Clip Art/Graphic Library file. Place a graphic on the clipboard/scrapbook by copying and pasting and by using an image capture program.

3 Know when an image is pasted in a document as a text character or as a graphic.

4 Change the location, size, and proportion of a graphic using the graphics handles. Align graphic objects.

5 Understand and use text wrap on a graphics object.

6 Draw a box or circle around text.

7 Select a line size.

8 Create a movable text box.

9 Create a three-slide presentation with a graphic on each slide (ClarisWorks only):
- create page breaks
- change view
- select fade

10 Know and use WordArt (Microsoft Word only)

11 Use a template to create a certificate of achievement for a student.

YOUR PORTFOLIO MUST INCLUDE BOTH THE PRINTOUT AND FILE OF A SAMPLE WORKSHEET OR PARENT COMMUNICATION THAT DEMONSTRATES:

1. Three simple, original graphics that are aligned and grouped

2. a piece of clip art that the text wraps around

3. a graphic that has been copied and resized to be 50% larger or smaller than the original

4. a movable text box with a border

➤ TEACHER NEED FOR BASIC GRAPHICS SKILLS

Teachers know that pictures are often worth more than even a 1,000 words when trying to explain a difficult concept. Good graphic images in handouts or presentations:

▶ provide information

▶ illustrate ideas

▶ create interest

▶ help visual learners

▶ provide memory aids

▶ emphasize or set off important ideas or concepts

Teachers also can use graphics to create professional looking banners, newsletters, posters, bookmarks, banners, nametags, signs, buttons, and certificates for a fraction of the cost of commercial ones. Graphics in letters to parents can help create the interest that increases the likelihood they will be read.

 FREE ADVICE: *For ideas on how to make your work look very professional, read Robin Williams' two short, but excellent books:*

The Mac (PC) Is Not a Typewriter. *Peachpit Press, 1990.*

The Non-Designer's Design Book. *Peachpit Press, 1994.*

 HOMEWORK: Use graphics tools to create a floor plan of your classroom. Include spaces for student names in seating locations so that the printout can be used as a seating chart.

or

Use the graphics features to create a classroom newsletter that includes images, drawings, and charts.

➤ STUDENT NEED FOR BASIC GRAPHICS SKILLS

Student projects can be more effective and more enjoyable when the information in them is communicated visually as well as verbally. Students can and should know how to create the same materials as teachers. History reports that take the format of newspapers or science projects with diagrams are common ways students use graphics with a word processor or desktop publishing program.

ADVANCED GRAPHICS SKILLS

1. Convert graphic files so that they can be used in Web pages.

2. Use filters to create special effects.

3. Use a scanner to digitize photographs or drawings.

4. Use a digital camera and import its images into a document.

VI Student Assessment

SELF-ASSESSMENT

LEVEL 1   I do not use the computer for student assessment.

LEVEL 2   I understand that there are ways I can keep track of student progress using the computer. I keep some student-produced materials on the computer and write evaluations of student work and notes to parents with the word processor.

LEVEL 3   I effectively use an electronic grade book to keep track of student data or I keep portfolios of student-produced materials on the computer. I use the electronic data during parent/teacher conferences.

LEVEL 4   I rely on the computer to keep track of outcomes and objectives individual students have mastered. I use that information in determining assignments, teaching strategies, and groupings.

CLASS OBJECTIVES: STUDENT ASSESSMENT (3 HOURS)

Using a commercial grade book program, the module of a student management program, or a custom designed spreadsheet:

1   Create a class file.

2   Enter student names.

3   Create graded criteria for:
- homework
- quizzes, tests, final tests
- projects
- extra credit

4   Establish weights for graded criteria.

5   Create a grading scale.

6   Calculate final grades.

7   Print individual student reports.

8   Calculate class statistics.

9   Chart or graph class statistics.

10   Prepare grade book for another grading period.

YOUR PORTFOLIO MUST INCLUDE BOTH THE PRINTOUT AND FILE OF AN ELECTRONIC GRADE BOOK THAT SHOWS:

1. student names
2. assignments
3. an assignment value system/grading scale

ADVANCED SKILLS:

1. Export records.
2. Create printed checklists from grade book class list.
3. Examine electronic portfolio systems for assessing and archiving student work.
4. Develop an online grade book accessible by student for parents.

TEACHER NEED FOR BASIC GRADE KEEPING SKILLS

For most teachers, using an automated grade book is a natural first use of the computer. Data a teacher has already been keeping are now simply recorded and stored electronically. Many grade book programs are even designed to look like paper grade books with their grids of columns and rows.

The use of an electronic grade book offers several advantages:

▶ Importing student names and other data saves time.

▶ Inaccurate data caused by handwriting or math calculation can be reduced.

▶ Reports to parents and students are quickly prepared and easily read.

▶ Easily assigning weights to various assignments helps create a more accurate grading system.

Using electronic means of recording performance is coming at a time in which society is asking for higher accountability from its schools. Part of this accountability is providing the results of assessments of more specific, observable skills and knowledge. For example, knowing that a student received a *B* in English does not tell parents, potential employers, or the students themselves as much as a list of competencies that have been acquired in the course. For already overburdened teachers, semiautomation of the record keeping process may be not be an option.

 FREE ADVICE: *This is a good time to reinforce the ideas of data security, privacy, and maintaining good backup files.*

 HOMEWORK:
1. Install the electronic grade book program on your classroom computer.
2. Enter the class list.
3. Create at least three assignment types.
4. Develop a grading scale for your class.
5. Print a grade report for an individual student.

IMPLICATIONS FOR STUDENTS AND PARENTS

> **Parents become real teaching partners for their children.**

As the skills and knowledge expected of a student during a grade or class are refined and articulated, this information can be shared with parents to help them become real teaching partners for their children. When teachers can tell in precise and measurable ways what students need to be able to know and do by the end of a unit or course, parents can then provide practice opportunities, check assignments, and monitor progress.

Electronically stored data are also more accessible data. Individual student performance data moved to the Internet, accessible by password to ensure privacy, give parents the ability to learn their children's progress throughout the school term. No longer will the conference after six to nine weeks of school be the only means of determining the strengths and weaknesses a student may be developing. This is education in "real time."

VII Spreadsheet use

SELF-ASSESSMENT

LEVEL 1 I do not use a spreadsheet, nor can I identify any uses or features it might have that would benefit the way I work.

LEVEL 2 I understand the use of a spreadsheet and can navigate within one. I can create a simple spreadsheet that adds a column of numbers.

LEVEL 3 I use a spreadsheet for several applications. These spreadsheets use labels, formulas, and cell references. I can change the format of the spreadsheets by changing column widths and text style. I can use the spreadsheet to make a simple graph or chart.

LEVEL 4 I use the spreadsheet not only for my work but with students to help them improve their own data-keeping and analysis skills.

 ## CLASS OBJECTIVES: BEGINNING SPREADSHEETS (3 HOURS)

1 Understand the function of the spreadsheet.

2 Open a new spreadsheet and identify rows, columns, and cells.

3 Know and use labels, values, and formulas.

4 Use a range of values in a formula.

5 Add additional rows and columns.

6 Change the width of columns.

7 Alphabetize items in a spreadsheet.

8 Format spreadsheet cells, rows, and columns / format numbers as currency.

9 Create and size a chart on the spreadsheet.

10 Paste a chart into a word processing document.

11 Delete column and row headings and grid lines. Restore the same.

12 Select a print range.

13 Select a horizontal print orientation.

 ### YOUR PORTFOLIO MUST INCLUDE BOTH THE PRINTOUT AND FILE OF A SPREADSHEET THAT DEMONSTRATES:

1. the use of column and row labels, a cell reference and formula that uses a range of cells

2. a variety of column widths and text styles

3. a simple, well-labeled pie or bar chart that uses data in the spreadsheet

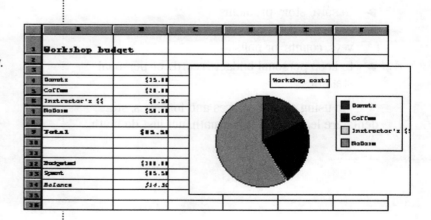

TEACHER NEED FOR BASIC SPREADSHEET SKILLS

Spreadsheets are a practical way to keep and work with numerical data in an organized, easily read, and accurate way. Many nonmathematical people have found that spreadsheets can take the drudgery out of calculations. Well-designed printed reports generated by the spreadsheet are rapidly understood and, I think, are more readily believed.

► Most teachers are responsible for some budget keeping. Revenues and expenses are easily and accurately kept using a simple spreadsheet. (You can catch your business office's mistakes.)
- ▪ fundraising sales
- ▪ classroom materials budget
- ▪ extracurricular activities budgets

► Spreadsheets can be modified to create highly customized grade books. Progress charts and checklist forms can be made using a spreadsheet grid.

► Coaches and athletic directors use spreadsheets to record sports statistics.

► The results of any data-gathering projects – surveys, counts, and polls – can be organized and graphed.

STUDENT NEED FOR BASIC SPREADSHEET SKILLS

Besides benefiting from more accurate record keeping by teachers, students can use the spreadsheet in a wide variety of classroom activities:

► to solve story problems
► to record data from projects that involve surveys, counts, or polls
► to keep personal budget records or personal statistics

In using cell references and formulas, students are learning to think math, not just do math.

 HOMEWORK: Create a spreadsheet for these problems:

1. Develop a favorite food graph for your class.

2. You are in charge of the school play. You have a budget of $500. You expect to take in $200 in ticket sales. Here are your expenses:

scripts and royalties	$237.45
set materials	$101.67
costume rental	$57.34

Create a spreadsheet that gives you a running total of your balance.

3. Here is a story problem your kids can solve using the spreadsheet:

Farmer Brown wants to raise chickens. However, she must first build some chicken coops. Brown plans to raise 150 chickens, and each coop can hold 50 chickens. To build a coop takes 75 feet of board at $1.50 per board foot; 4 bundles of shingles at $20 per bundle; and 3 pounds of nails at $6 per pound. She also needs a gallon of paint which sells in a two-gallon can for $12 per gallon. How much money will Farmer Brown need to build the coops she needs? How much would she have to spend if she wants to raise 200 chickens? 500 chickens?

VIII Database use

SELF-ASSESSMENT

LEVEL 1 I do not use a database, nor can I identify any uses or features one might have that would benefit the way I work.

LEVEL 2 I understand the use of a database and can locate information within a premade database. I can add or delete data in a database.

LEVEL 3 I use databases for personal applications. I can create an original database—defining fields and creating layouts. I can find, sort, and print information in layouts that are clear and useful to me.

LEVEL 4 I can use formulas with my database to create summaries of numerical data. I can use database information to do a mail merge in a word processing document. I use the database not only for my work but with students to help them improve their own data keeping and analysis skills.

CLASS OBJECTIVES: USING A DATABASE (3 HOURS)

1 Understand the function of a database and give three examples of paper databases and three examples of electronic databases. Open and examine a premade database. Understand the concepts of:
  - record
  - field and field name
  - layout

2 Find records with specific information.

3 Add a new record to the database and enter data.

4 Update information in the database.

5 Create a new field.

6 Examine parts of a layout.

7 Insert a field in a layout.

YOUR PORTFOLIO MUST INCLUDE THE FILE OF AN ORIGINAL DATABASE THAT HAS:

1. at least 10 records of at least five fields

2. at least three layouts, including one label layout

3. printouts that show the information sorted in at least two ways

8 Arrange fields in a layout.

9 Prepare a layout for printing.

10 Sort records.

11 Print a database.

12 Create and modify a new layout.

CLASS OBJECTIVES:
CREATING A DATABASE (3 HOURS)

1 Design on paper an original database.

2 Open a new database and create fields.

3 Know the properties of these types of fields:
- text
- container
- number
- calculation
- date
- summary
- time
- global

4 Modify a layout.
- Know the parts: header, body, and footer and how to change their sizes.
- Arrange fields in a layout.
- Use the Align and Size features on fields.

5 Create layouts. Know the layout types: standard, blank, columnar, and labels.

6 Insert a field in a layout.

7 Create a new field.

8 Create a "pop-up" menu field.

9 Create a button.

10 Write a simple script.

 HOMEWORK: Design a database that could serve as an inventory for the items in your home or classroom. Create the form on paper first. Decide if any of the fields need to be numerical or calculations. Design a columnar layout that would provide a list of items and their value for your insurance company.

11 Access the help menu and tutorial.

12 Set users and a password for your database.

13 Locate and open the district's database server.

14 Understand the applications for which the district is using databases.

ADVANCED DATABASE SKILLS:

1. Create a database that can be accessed over a network by multiple users.

2. Create a database than can be accessed via the World Wide Web.

3. Work with Avery preset labels.

▶ TEACHER NEED FOR BASIC DATABASE SKILLS

Information in a digital format is increasingly being kept in readily searchable databases. Companies from which we purchase products use databases to track our tastes as well as our addresses; airline schedules are giant databases, as are library catalogs and full-text magazine indexes. Schools are using databases for purchasing, inventories, and district-wide student record keeping. We are using databases when we search for information on the Internet.

Teachers can use this somewhat complex software in powerful ways. First they need to be able to do accurate searches in the ready-made databases mentioned above, not just to find information, but to analyze trends.

Student records, including basic data, progress reporting, discipline, individualized learning plans,

> **Curricula and teaching resources can be made available in database form.**

and health records, can be tracked using either self-made or commercial databases. (A powerful skill is to be able to export data from a commercial database into a self-made database or spreadsheet where it can be viewed and used for individual purposes.) Curricula and teaching resources can be made available in database form. Networking has made it possible for large numbers of people to access information from any location in a district. Using an intranet accessible from the Internet makes information available to teachers from home and by parents.

A reasonable, long-term goal for many districts is to replace all paper forms with electronic systems. Most of these systems will be databases. (See diagram, below.)

▶ STUDENT NEED FOR BASIC DATABASE SKILLS

A good understanding of how databases work will increase the efficacy with which students can find information in them.

Databases used as part of student projects are excellent ways to help students not only store information, but categorize, sort, analyze, and communicate it. Student projects that make use of original databases include collecting and organizing information about:

- presidents
- states
- product features

Students, like teachers, can use personal databases for inventories of collections, addresses, reviews, or recipes.

FREE ADVICE: Good instruction in database use addresses issues of data privacy.

Using pre-made templates that come with most databases is a good way to quickly create a useful, sophisticated database.

For long-term use, look for databases that are cross-platform, are usable by multiple users over a network, and are accessible from web page interfaces.

A SAMPLE DISTRICT DATABASE PLAN

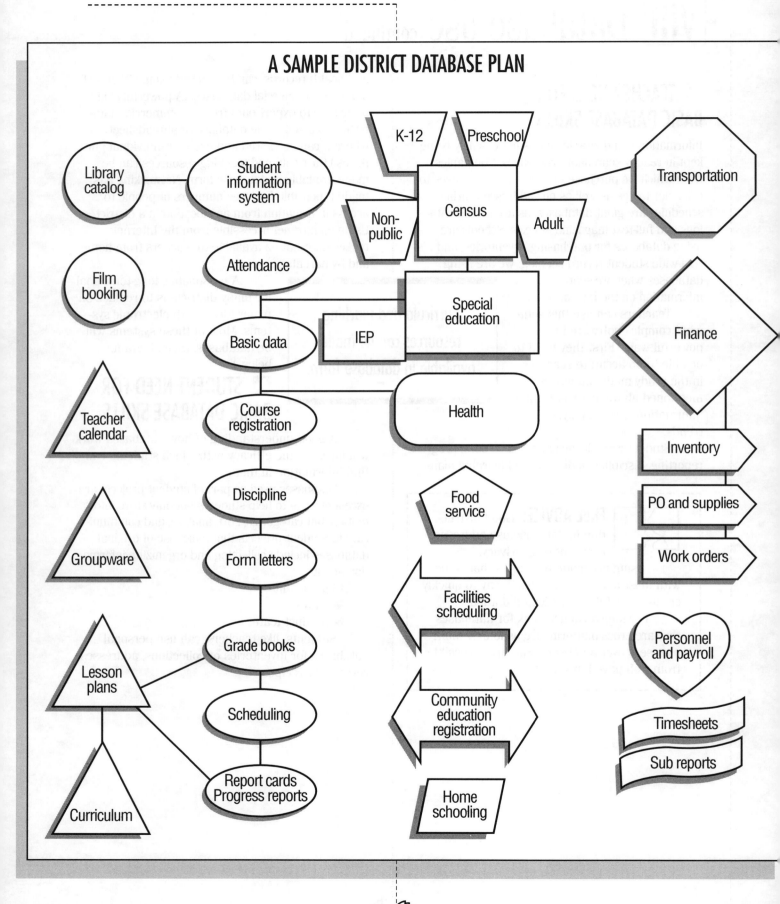

IX Hypermedia use

SELF-ASSESSMENT

LEVEL 1   I do not use hypermedia (HyperStudio), nor can I identify any uses or features it might have that would benefit the way I work.

LEVEL 2   I can navigate through a premade hypermedia program.

LEVEL 3   I can create my own hypermedia stacks for information presentation. These stacks use navigation buttons, sounds, dissolves, graphics, and text fields. I can use an LCD projection device to display the presentation to a class.

LEVEL 4   I use hypermedia with students who are making their own stacks for information keeping and presentation.

CLASS OBJECTIVES: CREATING A HYPERMEDIA STACK (3 HOURS)

1 Understand the features, uses, advantages, and disadvantages of hypermedia programs and projects.

2 Using a premade hypermedia stack:
- open the stack
- use buttons to navigate through the stack
- navigate to the "home" card
- open a second stack

3 Create an original stack by:
- storyboarding a stack on paper
- creating a new file
- selecting/creating a background
- adding text
- adding graphics/clip art
- adding sounds
- adding digital movie clips
- adding new cards to the stack
- adding buttons that move the reader from card to card
- creating transitions (wipes, fades, sounds) between cards

4 Use the special features (in Hyperstudio)

5 Save the stack. Understand how the stack can be shared using the "player" program.

YOUR PORTFOLIO MUST INCLUDE BOTH PRINTOUT AND FILE OF A MULTIMEDIA STACK THAT DEMONSTRATES:

1. three cards on a related topic linked to a homecard using clearly labeled buttons
2. a piece of clip art placed on the background that appears on each card
3. a text field and a graphic on each card
4. at least one example of a sound and video clip in the stack
5. the use of special transition effects and sounds when moving from card to card

ADVANCED SKILLS:

1. Create links within the stack to external resources such as other stacks, other programs, or Internet sites.
2. Create animations in your stack.
3. Digitize original video for use in the stack.

TEACHER NEED FOR BASIC HYPERMEDIA SKILLS

Teachers can use a program like HyperStudio as a presentation tool (electronic slide shows to accompany lessons) and as tool to create on-screen tutorials and lessons. The ease with which text, original graphics, clip art, photographs, sounds, animations, digitized movies, and now Web sources can be combined gives multimedia the potential to be a very powerful teaching tool.

Currently, this computer application at its most sophisticated level is the most hardware demanding. Fast processors, lots of RAM and hard drive space, and special equipment to digitize photographs, movies, and sound are all essential. Very basic stacks, using original artwork and the multimedia resources included with most hypermedia programs, can be created with basic equipment. (HyperStudio began as a program for the Apple II computer!)

Many teachers for their professional use may wish to use a more sophisticated presentation program like PowerPoint to accompany lectures or lessons. Working from an outline, teachers can quickly create electronic slides that incorporate many of the elements of a multimedia program. Special effects like animated text builds and charts can both enhance the message and increase audience attention.

Finally, teachers need to understand the basics of multimedia production so they can assist students who are using this powerful new information-processing tool.

HOMEWORK: Create a stack of at least five cards that tell about you as a teacher that you can share with your students.

STUDENT NEED FOR BASIC HYPERMEDIA SKILLS

Increasingly, teachers are encouraging students to report research findings in a multimedia format. The amount and variety of information about a topic dramatically increase when students use a variety of information formats (text, photos, graphs, sounds, movies), but creating, organizing, and designing navigation paths through stacks demands that their creators think about classifying and organizing their data.

Other uses of hypermedia programs besides reporting and presenting include:
- creating games
- recording journals
- writing illustrated, interactive stories

FREE ADVICE: *Good assessment of student hypermedia projects will have two strands of quality criteria: a content strand and a production strand. Too many hypermedia projects are very glitzy, but contain little or poor content.*

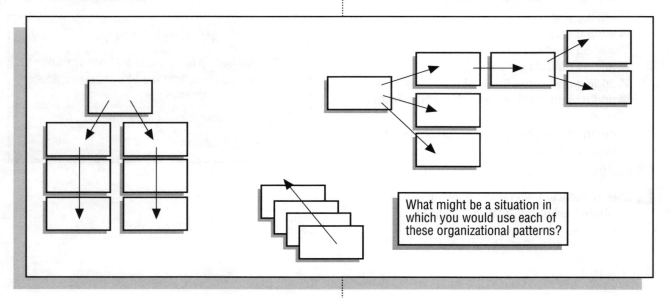

What might be a situation in which you would use each of these organizational patterns?

X Ethical use

SELF-ASSESSMENT

LEVEL 1   I am not aware of any ethical issues surrounding computer use.

LEVEL 2   I know some copyright restrictions apply to computer software.

LEVEL 3   I clearly understand the difference between freeware, shareware, and commercial software and the fees involved in the use of each. I know the programs for which the district or my building holds a site license. I understand the school board policy on the use of copyrighted materials. I demonstrate ethical usage of all software and let my students know my personal stand on legal and moral issues involving technology. I know and enforce the school's technology policies and guidelines, including its Internet acceptable use policy. I have a personal philosophy I can articulate regarding the use of technology in education.

LEVEL 4   I am aware of other controversial aspects of technology use, including data privacy, equitable access, and free speech issues. I can speak to a variety of technology issues at my professional association meetings, to parent groups, and to the general community.

CLASS OJECTIVE: ETHICAL USE

This information and these skills are best taught as a part of the training sessions to which they can be immediately applied.

Basic Computer Operation

1 Know computer care basics.

2 Understand legal and illegal uses of software.

3 Understand ethical and unethical uses of school equipment

4 Understand how computer viruses are contracted, avoided, and eliminated.

File Management, Database Use, and Student Assessment

5 Know how data can be secured and privacy protected.

Graphics Use, Hypermedia Use, World Wide Web Use

6 Understand copyright issues regarding clip art, fonts, and materials obtained from the Internet.

E-mail

7 Understand the basics of Internet netiquette.

World Wide Web Use

8 Know the district's acceptable use policy for network and Internet use.

YOUR PORTFOLIO MUST INCLUDE A WORD-PROCESSED STATEMENT NO LONGER THAN TWO PAGES OF:

1. your personal philosophy of the use of technology in education

2. a definition and example of freeware, shareware, and commercial software

3. a copy of the district's Internet and copyright policies.

⯈ TEACHER NEED FOR UNDERSTANDING OF BASIC ETHICAL USE ISSUES

Why do technology ethics deserve special attention? There is a variety of reasons:

▶ Using technology to communicate and operate in a "virtual world," one that only exists within computers and computer networks, is a new phenomenon that is not always well understood by many teachers who received their primary education prior to its existence.

 ■ Our new technological capabilities also may require new ethical considerations.

 ■ The ability to send unsolicited commercial messages to millions of people (spamming) was not possible before there was e-mail or the Internet.

 ■ Digital photography has made the manipulation of images undetectable, an impossible feat with chemical photography.

 ■ Prior to the Internet, minors faced physical barriers of access to sexually explicit materials.

 ■ Intellectual property in digital format can now be duplicated with incredible ease.

▶ There is the temptation to view one's actions in the intangible, virtual world of information technologies as being less serious than one's actions in the real world. Information technology misuse by many people, especially the young, is viewed as a low-risk, game-like challenge.

Not long ago, ethical technology questions were only of interest to a very few specialists. But as the use of information technologies spreads throughout society and its importance to our national economies and individual careers grows, everyone will need to make appropriate ethical decisions when using computers. Studies show that persons involved in computer crimes acquire both their interest and skills at an early age.

Teachers need to know the ethical issues of technology and be able to conduct informed discussions with students as a part of regular technology training and when technology misuse occurs. Perhaps even more importantly, teachers need to demonstrate the ethical use of technologies. Effective monitoring of student activities cannot occur unless the teacher knows of possible actions that are ethically and legally improper.

Applied ethics needs to be an integral part of technology use in schools. Technology, especially electronic communications, has proven to be a tempting medium for new types of mischief, vandalism, and other, more serious crimes. Early education about the ethical use of technologies may help stem the abuse of those technologies as students grow older.

Students also need the chance to discuss how technology will impact the society and culture in which they live. Concepts of privacy, property, and appropriateness are often difficult for teachers to approach since the values inherent in them can interpreted quite differently—even within a single school system, depending on its families' religious and political beliefs. This difficulty cannot be used as an excuse to avoid such issues. One responsible approach is to deal with ethical issues in the context of civics instruction.

> **Everyone will need to make appropriate ethical decisions when using computers.**

FREE ADVICE: *Distribute copies of your district's acceptable use policy, copyright policies, and other relevant documents during the first training session and ask that they be included in all portfolios.*

While an entire school or district may wish to use a single set of guidelines, each classroom teacher needs to understand, teach, and model the guidelines. Simple rules, easily remembered by children, are probably the best:

JOHNSON'S THREE P'S OF TECHNOLOGY ETHICS:

1 *Privacy: I will protect my privacy and respect the privacy of others.*

2 *Property: I will protect my property and respect the property of others.*

3 *a(P)propriate Use: I will use technology in constructive ways and in ways that do not break the rules of my family, church, school, or government.*

CHAPTER 3

Internet Skills for Teachers

 The Internet is the earliest manifestation of how business will be conducted from now on.
—Fortune Magazine, *1995.*

I have used variations of these rubrics working with teachers and media specialists over the past six years. Big changes in organization, software, and resources have required regular revisions to the skills needed to use the Internet effectively.

Not long ago, various means of storing information on the Internet required a variety of specialized tools for finding and accessing it. Tools like gophers, newsreaders, e-mail programs, Telnet, and FTP were dedicated to single tasks. Now most resources can be accessed using an Internet browser such as Netscape or Explorer. The specialized tools have become modules built in to these powerful programs. For all but the most demanding of users, a Web browser configured with some helper applications is the only tool needed to access the Internet.

The interface to the Internet has changed dramatically as well. Once the Internet was accessed almost exclusively through text-based interfaces running on large computers to which one's workstation only served as a "dumb terminal." This model of access has been largely replaced by workstation-based programs that use the workstation's processing power to provide point-and-click simplicity of use and to display information in colorful formats that include text styles and fonts, graphics, sounds, animations, and digital video. "Streaming" is quickly allowing Internet users to play music and hear discussions. Using the Internet as a telephone is becoming more common. "Push" technologies deliver up-to-the-minute news, weather, and business information right to the desktop, relieving the user the responsibility of finding and retrieving that information.

These improvements have allowed Internet instructional time to be spent less wondering:

▶ How do I find information?

▶ How do I use the access tools?

▶ How do I download the information?

and more evaluating:

▶ How can I focus my searches?

▶ How can I determine if the information is accurate?

▶ How do I interpret and make meaning of the information?

▶ How do I use and communicate the information?

▶ How do I prepare my information so it can be displayed on the Internet?

Believe me, the older skills, while at times frustrating to teach, were easier to master!

Needed skills for using the Internet seem to change almost daily, but these rubrics can be used as a starting point.

Each of the Internet rubrics has four levels:

LEVEL 1: Pre-awareness
LEVEL 2: Awareness
LEVEL 3: Mastery
LEVEL 4: Advanced

Prior to training, we assume most teachers are at level 1 or 2, and our training efforts are designed with that assumption. By the end of the training, we anticipate teachers will be at level 3 or 4 in most skill areas and will have gone up at least one level in all areas.

These rubrics then serve two purposes: By asking teachers to complete an anonymous self-assessment using the rubrics before training and again after training, we can judge the effectiveness of our staff development efforts. Simple graphs showing the percentage of training participants at each level pre- and post-training are constructed. (See Chapter Five, "Assess Staff Development.") These results can be shared with the staff development committees and administration.

The rubrics also provide a road map for teachers wanting to improve their Internet skills. By examining the specific skills described, teachers know in what areas they need to continue to take classes or practice.

Below are the instructions to teachers for completing a self-assessment and the rubrics themselves. Following each rubric is:

▶ a checklist of specific objectives that can be met for most new computer users in a three- to four-hour training session

▶ items a teacher portfolio should include that would demonstrate competency

▶ a short commentary on the uses to which a teacher may put this skill and possible uses it might have in the classroom

▶ when appropriate, free advice about teaching the skill

Please feel free to use and modify the rubrics for your district's specific needs and as technology changes.

▶ TEACHER INSTRUCTIONS FOR INTERNET SKILLS RUBRICS

This is an anonymous assessment. You do not need to sign the pre- or post-evaluation tool. Individual results wil be aggregated to determine how effective the program has been for the group as a whole. You should, however, keep track of your own individual progress.

Please judge your level of achievement in each of the following competencies. Circle the number that best reflects your current level of skill attainment. (Be honest, but be kind.) At the end of the training program, you will complete the same set of rubrics, which will reflect your level of skill attainment at that time; level 3 is considered mastery. This tool is to help measure the effectiveness of our training program and help you do a self-analysis to determine the areas in which you should continue to learn and practice. Keep a copy of these rubrics to refer to during the training.

◨ Internet basics

SELF-ASSESSMENT

LEVEL 1 I do not understand how networks work, nor can I identify any personal or professional uses for networks, including the Internet. I do not have an account on any network, nor would I know how to get one.

LEVEL 2 I can identify some personal or professional uses for networks, and understand they have a value to my students and me. I've read some articles about the Internet in the popular press. I can directly use network access to a library catalog or CD-ROM.

LEVEL 3 I can describe what a computer network does and how it can be useful personally and professionally. I can distinguish between a local area network, a wide area network, and the Internet and can describe educational uses for each. I can describe the history of the Internet and recognize its international character, and I know to a degree the extent of its resources. I have personal access to the Internet that allows me to receive and send e-mail, download files, and access the World Wide Web. I know I must protect my password and should restrict access by others to my account.

LEVEL 4 I use networks on a daily basis to access and communicate information. I can serve as an active participant in a school or organizational planning group, giving advice and providing information about networks. I can recommend several ways of obtaining Internet access to others.

CLASS OBJECTIVES: INTERNET BASICS (3 HOURS)

1 Know the purpose of, define, and give personal and professional uses for and resources available on:

- local area networks
- wide area networks
- the Internet

2 Know the meanings of the terms and acronyms:

- AUP
- ASCII files/binary files
- CGI
- Chat/MUD/MOO
- Clients and servers
- EFF
- FAQS
- File compression
- FTP
- Frame relay/ISDN
- HTTP/HTML
- TCP/IP
- Helper applications
- Intranet
- URL
- Mailing list/listserv
- Modem
- Netiquette
- Router
- Search engine
- Usenet news
- Virus (computer)

3 Know the difference between Internet access using terminal emulation and SLIP/PPP and the difference between dial-up connections and direct network connections. Know the equipment and software needed for the type of connection and which types you will primarily be using. Know the steps for making a connection to the Internet. Identify a desirable speed of connection to the Internet.

4 Know your account name and password, the name of your Internet service provider, and the URL for your school's Web site. Understand password and network security procedures.

YOUR PORTFOLIO MIGHT INCLUDE:

1. a one-page glossary of Internet terms
2. three one-paragraph summaries of book chapters or magazine articles about the history and structure of the Internet
3. a description of how you, as a user, gain Internet access

HOMEWORK: Test your network connection from your classroom or home.

➤ WHY TEACHERS NEED AN UNDERSTANDING OF BACKGROUND INFORMATION ABOUT THE INTERNET

In its current incarnation, the Information Superhighway is often frustrating to use and expensive to take into classrooms. It contains materials that no teacher wants students to read, its content is mostly unedited and often unreliable, and no one has demonstrated that its presence in a classroom improves student learning.

Yet between 1994 and 1998, the number of school districts with access to the Internet has increased from about 200 to well over 2,000. Federal and national initiatives are providing funding for connectivity, and many parents are excited and insistent that their children learn how to use this resource.

Why do schools need to connect to the Internet and why do teachers need to be proficient in its use?

➤ **OUR CHILDREN WILL NEED TO BE ABLE USE THE INTERNET TO COMPETE IN BUSINESS AND COLLEGE.** Commercial accounts are now the fastest growing segment of the network. Just as businesses that do not effectively use networks will not survive in tomorrow's economy, children who can't telecommunicate will not survive in tomorrow's businesses. Universities have long used the Internet, and access for students is now a given at most of them. Students will be expected to use the Internet to access scholarly journals, research library catalogs and extensive databases, and to communicate with experts and colleagues worldwide.

➤ **THE INTERNET IS AN IMPORTANT RESOURCE THAT CAN IMPROVE CURRENT TEACHING PRACTICES.** Like all technologies, the Internet can be a wonderful resource for helping teachers create activities that include the purposeful use of current informa-

> # Our children will need to be able use the Internet to compete in business and college.

tion. Business community surveys have shown a demand for future workers, from executives to mail clerks, who are able to apply knowledge to new situations and become creative problem solvers. "Basic" skills now include the ability to find, evaluate, and use information—and information increasingly moves over wires.

➤ **OUR CHILDREN WILL NEED TO BE ABLE TO USE THE INTERNET AS INFORMED, RESPONSIBLE CITIZENS.** Regardless of whether one regards the government as the problem or the solution, access to it and the information it generates is vital if a citizen is to fully participate in the democratic process. Government at all levels is moving toward doing business electronically. The private news sector too does much of its communicating online. *Minneapolis Star Tribune*'s electronic edition offers over three times the depth of coverage of its print edition. Internet users find their most timely information in electronic journals. And increasingly, information will be available only in an electronic format. Citizens need reliable information to make good decisions about how their society is run. For our children, that will be impossible without electronic information skills and access.

In his book *Savage Inequalities,* Jonathan Kozol warns that our society has two kinds of schools: those for the governors and those for the governed. Resource-poor schools have less chance of developing critical thinkers, creative problem solvers, and self-governing citizens. The Internet is a vital educational resource if we are to graduate well-paid button programmers rather than minimum-wage button pushers.

Internet access by itself will not help students. Well-trained teachers who can use the Internet as a teaching tool are critical to its effective use. Teachers need to know the extent of the resources available on networks of all kinds, know how and why computer networking has evolved, and have a working vocabulary of networking and Internet terminology. They also need to know how to get professional and personal access to their institution's networks and the Internet.

FREE ADVICE: *Always check network connections before a class. Help teachers understand that the speed with which one can access the Internet is dependent on the amount of traffic and often the time of day.*

► II E-mail and Electronic Mailing Lists

SELF-ASSESSMENT

LEVEL 1 I do not use e-mail.

LEVEL 2 I understand the concept of e-mail and can explain some administrative and educational uses for it.

LEVEL 3 I use e-mail regularly and can
- ► read and delete messages
- ► send, forward, and reply to messages
- ► create nicknames, mailing lists, and a signature file
- ► send and receive attachments
- ► use electronic mailing lists and understand the professional uses of them
- ► read and contribute to a professional electronic mailing list

LEVEL 4 I can send group mailings and feel confident that I could administer an electronic mailing list. I use activities in my teaching that require e-mail. I can locate lists of subject-oriented mailing lists.

CLASS OBJECTIVES: E-mail (3 hours)

1 Identify and open the e-mail program.

2 Check and configure settings. Know and understand username, e-mail address, and password.

3 Get new mail. Identify the time and date, e-mail address of the sender, and subject of an e-mail message.

4 Read and delete a message.

5 Send a message. Send a carbon copy of a message.

6 Reply to a message, forward a message, and print a message.

7 Create a nickname file and set up a nickname with multiple addresses.

8 Create a signature file and understand the elements of a good signature file.

9 Organize and store sent and received messages.

10 Understand rules governing the polite use of e-mail (netiquette).

ADVANCED SKILLS:

1. Send, receive, and open attachments.
2. Subscribe, unsubscribe, and send a message to the district's electronic mailing list.
3. Use search tools to locate e-mail addresses.
4. Use filters to sort incoming messages.
5. Locate sources of student projects that use e-mail.

YOUR PORTFOLIO MIGHT INCLUDE:

1. the printout of an e-mail that you have sent and an e-mail that you have received
2. a printout of your signature file
3. a printout of several messages from an electronic mailing list

WHY TEACHERS NEED BASIC E-MAIL SKILLS:

As educators become more comfortable with e-mail, a pattern of growth emerges:

1 PERSONAL USE. Many teachers begin using e-mail because they have a child (often in college), friend or professional colleague who has an e-mail account. The personal nature of the correspondence makes using the computer compelling enough to begin mastering its basic operation.

2 CONDUCTING SCHOOL BUSINESS. Using e-mail for certain tasks is becoming standard operating procedure in schools that have adequate resources. Once all teachers have networked computers on their desks, the school bulletin, departmental information, class attendance-

> Using e-mail for certain tasks is becoming standard operating procedure in schools that have adequate resources.

FREE ADVICE: *Beginning e-mail users need recipe-type instruction lists and hands-on classes—not just on using the e-mail program, but also about general computer operations such as opening applications and files, text editing, using a mouse, and even keyboarding. This is why lots of time needs to be budgeted for "e-mail instruction."*

Among the skills users most appreciate learning is how to determine if a bounced message is caused by a faulty address or by network problems.

One source of potential frustration for new e-mail users is the precision with which e-mail addresses need to be typed. Unlike human postal workers, computers need 100% address accuracy. The lower case letter L cannot substitute for the numeral 1. A dot (period) at the end of an address will cause the message to bounce, as will any spaces in an address. New e-mail users may need to be taught how to say their addresses.

Lessons in online netiquette need to be taught at the same time as the network skills themselves.

HOMEWORK: Send at least three e-mail messages to associates, and print out their responses.

Subscribe to the *Word of the Day* newsletter: Send an e-mail to **word-of-the-day@parlez.net** with "subscribe" as the subject. (Please make sure your return address is correctly configured in your browser!) Or simply fill out the subscription form at **<http://www.parlez.com/word-of-the-day/>**. Subscriptions are free.

reporting, team-planning, and parent communications all can effectively be done electronically.

3 OBTAINING INFORMATION. Educators soon find there is a wealth of information to be obtained using their e-mail accounts. Discussion lists, electronic magazines and journals, and daily quotes, jokes, and vocabulary words can keep the reader current on almost any topic. Customized news feeds can be sent to a teacher's desktop each day using services such as InfoBeat **<http://www.infobeat.com>**.

4 CREATING CLASSROOM ACTIVITIES. As many classroom teachers get excited about how e-mail has provided them with new learning opportunities, they will be anxious to get their students using this resource productively. Judy Harris' wonderful book *Way of the Ferret: Finding Educational Resources on the Internet* (ISTE, 2nd ed. 1995) and Al Rogers' exciting Global Schoolhouse Network Web site **<http://www.gsn.org/>** and its HILITES mailing list are invaluable sources about these kinds of projects.

III The World Wide Web

SELF-ASSESSMENT

LEVEL 1   I do not use the World Wide Web.

LEVEL 2   I am aware that the World Wide Web is a means of sharing information on the Internet. I can browse the Web for recreational purposes.

LEVEL 3   I can use a Web browser such as Explorer or Netscape to find information on the World Wide Web and can list some of the Web's unique features. I can explain the terms hypertext, URL, HTTP, and HTML. I can write URLs to share information locations with others. I can use Web search engines to locate subject specific information and can create bookmarks to Web sites of educational value.

LEVEL 4   I can configure my Web browser with a variety of helper applications. I understand what "cookies" do and whether to keep them enabled. I can speak to the security issues of online commerce and data privacy.

 ## CLASS OBJECTIVES: WORLD WIDE WEB (3 HOURS)

1 Understand the unique properties of the World Wide Web.

2 Know what a Web browser does. Know the brand names of at least two popular browsers and how to obtain recent versions of them.

3 Configure the browser to a home page and configure e-mail settings.

4 Show the location bar. Directly enter a URL for a location.

5 Use page links to navigate through the Web.

6 Know the functions of the tool bar items on the browser.

7 Use forward and back buttons and search history to navigate.

8 Use a search engine to locate information on a topic.

9 Print a page from the WWW.

10 Create bookmarks. Arrange bookmarks.

11 Know and understand the district's acceptable use policy for Internet use.

ADVANCED SKILLS

Know what the following helper applications do, how to obtain them, and how to install them:

- Telnet
- FTP
- GIF converters
- Adobe Acrobat Reader
- Sound Machine
- QuickTime
- RealAudio
- Stuffit and UnZip

 ## YOUR PORTFOLIO MIGHT INCLUDE:

1. the printout of a Web page on a topic of educational interest

2. the printout of the findings of an Internet search of an education topic using Yahoo, Lycos, Excite, or a similar site

➤ WHY TEACHERS NEED BASIC WORLD WIDE WEB USE SKILLS

Graphic browsers such as Netscape and Explorer have done for the Internet what the Macintosh and Windows interfaces did for operating systems: take complex and confusing tasks and make them simple enough for everyone to use. It's a good thing, too, since storing information in digital formats and accessing it using a network is increasingly becoming the standard way of doing business.

The World Wide Web, of course, is a tremendous source of professional information:

► lesson plans, activities, and support materials
► links to online projects
► professional research
► educational journals and magazines
► state and local educational data
► news

Lots of books of Internet resources are being published for teachers, students, and parents.

Teachers can create bookmark "bibliographies" of curricular sources for their students. These can be either bookmark files or Web pages that include the addresses as links. Preselecting sites for students helps them get into the material faster. An extension of using Internet resources as classroom support materials involves moving the class itself on to the Web. High schools and colleges that are willing to become "virtual institutions" are offering online classes and coursework.

In addition to being a research source, the Web is a practical and effective means for teachers to provide information about their classes and programs. Just as a school district's Web server can help students, parents, and the public easily access current activity schedules, staff directories, lunch menus, and policies, teacher-created Web pages can help students access class assignments and handouts.

HOMEWORK: Find 10 Web sites on a single topic of interest to you or on an area of your curriculum. Create bookmarks to them.

The Web also can be an exciting way for students to share their work with a wide audience. Creative writing and art, results of student research, and products of other classroom activities can be displayed on a district's Web server for other students throughout the world to examine and react to. Students in teacher preparation programs have ready access to student work for practice evaluating.

Many students are finding the Internet to be a primary source of information. And nowhere is it more obvious that the teacher's role in the educational process is moving from being the "sage on the stage" to being the "guide by the side" than when students start using Internet resources to fulfill classroom assignments. Teacher questioning moves from simple recall questions about curricular topics to queries such as:

► "How did you find your information?"
► "Is it relevant to the problem you are trying to solve?"
► "Is the information reliable, accurate, up-to-date?"
► "What are the implications of this information to you, the community or the nation?"
► "How can you use this information and how can you effectively communicate it to others?"

Redefined teaching role? You bet. Is the new role as important or more important than the old one? You bet.

> In addition to being a research source, the Web is a practical and effective means for teachers to provide information about their classes and programs.

IV Search Tools

SELF-ASSESSMENT

LEVEL 1 I cannot locate any information on the Internet.

LEVEL 2 I can occasionally locate useful information on the Internet by browsing or through remembered sources.

LEVEL 3 I can conduct an efficient search of Internet resources using directories such as Yahoo or search engines such as Excite, Lycos, and Infoseek. I can use advanced search commands to specify and limit the number of hits I get. I can state some guidelines for evaluating the information I find on the Internet and can write a bibliographic citation for information I find.

LEVEL 4 I can identify some specialized search tools for finding software and e-mail addresses. I can speculate on future developments in online information searching, including "know-bots" and other kinds of intelligent search agents.

CLASS OBJECTIVES: SEARCH TOOLS (3 HOURS)

1 Know the functions of Internet directories and Internet search engines. Know the circumstances under which to use each. Know the URLs for:

- Yahoo
- Yahooligans
- Excite
- Lycos
- Infoseek
- AltaVista

2 Conduct a search by a single term, by a multiple-word term, and by multiple terms. Compare the results from three of the search engines above.

3 Conduct a search using the advanced features of at least two search engines. Understand the symbols used to group terms, indicate proper names, and searches of full-text or page headings only.

4 Create a bookmark folder and set bookmarks for at least 10 sites on a topic specific to your subject area. Know how to export the bookmarks to a text file or send the file so others can use it.

5 Develop criteria for evaluating the reliability of a Web site. These might include:

- currency
- authority
- Web sponsor
- objectivity

6 Know the proper forms of bibliographic citations to Web resources.

ADVANCED SKILLS

1. Know the special features and best uses of a variety of search engines. Find a source of search engine comparisons.

2. Know and use search engines to locate a particular type of information such as e-mail addresses, gopher sites, or software.

YOUR PORTFOLIO MIGHT INCLUDE:

1. an annotated list of 10 education-related URLs

2. a printout of the advanced search commands for a single search engine

3. a list of criteria one might use to determine the accuracy of information found as a result of the search

➤ WHY TEACHERS NEED BASIC INTERNET SEARCH SKILLS

The skills inherent in finding information have radically changed. Over the past several years, most schools have moved from being information deserts to information jungles.

The teachers and librarians who served as guides in information deserts were primarily concerned with helping students locate *any* information. Most of us can remember that sigh of relief when locating the required fifth source for a term paper that was built with information from books, encyclopedias, reference materials, magazine articles, and newspaper clippings from the vertical file. We didn't need to be terribly discriminating about these sources. The information in these secondary sources had all been subjected to at least some editorial process by their publishers, and teachers didn't spend much time advising students to look for datedness, authority, or bias.

With access to the Internet and other networked sources of information such as CD-ROM reference materials and full-text periodical indexes, students suddenly find themselves in an information

> The skills inherent in finding information have radically changed.

 HOMEWORK: Search for Internet resources on a single topic using three different search engines. Choose a favorite and tell why it worked the best for you.

---

jungle. Resources are everywhere. Now instead of worrying about finding a minimum number of sources for a research project, the task becomes one of narrowing and selecting from the hundreds of "hits" found with an Internet search. The teacher and librarian, now serving as guides, move from locating scarce resources to helping students evaluate and select from an overwhelming number of them.

The Internet is also a primarily unedited medium. The information accessible to students could have been placed on a Web server by a college professor, scientific researcher, government official, another student, a malicious crackpot, or a business's marketing department. (And yes, I realize these are not mutually exclusive descriptions.) The presentation of the information doesn't help the student researcher. Skill in design and expertise on a topic have no relation.

Teachers and librarians, then, have to learn and teach their students to:

- ▶ understand the range of resources available
- ▶ narrow the range of available resources (and perhaps narrow the focus of the research itself)
- ▶ identify keywords that are descriptive and specific
- ▶ use online search engines' special symbols, punctuation, and tools to focus searches on specific topics.
- ▶ quickly determine by annotation which hits are topically relevant
- ▶ analyze individual sites and pages for:
  - ■ currency
  - ■ authority
  - ■ bias

FREE ADVICE: *Read Paul Gilster's* Digital Literacy *(John Wiley & Sons, 1997). Among other good tips, Gilster suggests learning to use a single search engine very well.*

Check Dr. Don Descy's Mankato Home Page <http://www.lme.mankato.msus.edu/mankato/mankato.HTML> for a purposely created display of misinformation.

Many schools are adding commercial online databases of information, such as UMI's ProQuest, the Electric Library, Scholastic Online, and Groliers Online, that use the Internet as a means of access rather than a content source. These edited, selected sources reduce the amount of time students and teachers need to validate the accuracy of information.

V Newsgroups, Gophers, and Telnet

SELF-ASSESSMENT

LEVEL 1 I have no knowledge of newsgroups, gophers, or Telnet functions.

LEVEL 2 I know there are resources in a variety of formats available on the Internet but cannot confidently access them.

LEVEL 3 I read the newsgroups that interest me on a regular basis, and I can contribute to newsgroups. I understand the use of gophers and can locate several that help me. I can write directions to locating a gopher so others can find it as well. I can access remote computers, including remote library catalogs, through the Telnet command. I can find the help screens when emulating remote computers and can log off properly.

LEVEL 4 I know how to find, configure, and use the specialized tools for newsgroups, gophers, and Telnet access. I use the resources found in these areas with my students.

CLASS OBJECTIVES: NEWSGROUPS, GOPHERS, AND TELNET (3 HOURS)

1 Configure a Web browser to access the news server of the school's ISP and use it to:
- find a list of newsgroups
- navigate through the list
- find newsgroups for educational purposes
- read a posting and a thread and post a response or question to a newsgroup

2 Use the browser to locate information stored on a gopher site by using Veronica or Jughead search engines. Navigate through a gopher site and understand its hierarchical organization. Know symbols indicating file types on a gopher menu.

3 Configure and use a Telnet program to access a remote server and navigate through that server. Understand that the host's commands must be used to access a remote host by Telnet. Know how to access a help screen at a remote site. Understand how to log on anonymously.

4 Use Telnet to access:
- an online public or academic library catalog
- a public free-net
- a specialized information server such as the Geographic Name server

YOUR PORTFOLIO MIGHT INCLUDE:

1. the printout of a list of newsgroups that have professional relevance

2. the printout of a message you have contributed to a newsgroup and responses you have received to it

3. the printout of a gopher menu of educational materials and the URL for the site

4. the printout of a search of a remote library catalog

➤ WHY TEACHERS NEED NEWSGROUP, GOPHER, AND TELNET SKILLS

The growth of the hypertext-based World Wide Web has overshadowed some of the older, text-based modes of storing and retrieving information from the Internet. Still, knowing how to find and access information from newsgroups, gophers, and remote sites using Telnet remain useful skills.

Newsgroups, or more properly Usenet newsgroups, function much like thousands of bulletin boards all arranged by general topic. Users can freely read and post messages to these unmoderated forums. The major domains (large groupings) of newsgroups include:

- ▶ alt (new, uncertified groups)
- ▶ comp (computers)
- ▶ K12 (education)
- ▶ soc (social issues)
- ▶ news (information about the Internet itself)
- ▶ rec (recreation, hobbies, and the arts)
- ▶ sci (scientific research)
- ▶ talk (unmoderated, mostly uninformed discussion)

The usefulness of any single newsgroup can run from invaluable (comp.virus) to valueless (alt.bite-me) to crude and possibly legally obscene (alt.sex). This resource is a very mixed bag at best, but for teachers and students wishing to contact people with like interests for ideas, experiences, and advice, newgroups can be of real help.

FREE ADVICE: *To get fast and easy access to specific information in a newsgroup, use a Web browser to go to* **DejaNews** *<http://www.dejanews.com>.*

The secret to using a remote computer that has been accessed with Telnet is to read the help screens. By typing in a question mark or the word "help," you can call up a list of commands at most remote sites.

When asked what kind of terminal you wish to emulate, always choose VT100. Don't ask why. Just do it.

HOMEWORK:

1. Locate a K12 newsgroup for your subject area or job. Read the messages.

2. Telnet to your nearest public university and locate a book using the online library. Check to see if other databases of information are available online.

Access to newgroups is primarily through a newsreader, either a stand-alone program or one built in to a Web browser. In either case, teachers can select only those groups they wish to read. Not all Internet service providers carry all newsgroups, and the length of time a message remains available on a news server can vary.

Gopher was an early (1991) attempt to bring order and access to resources on the Internet. Text files, graphics, sounds, video clips, and links to other gophers placed on a gopher server are part of a hierarchical menu the user can access with such gopher programs as TurboGopher and HGopher. A specialized search engine called Veronica allows the user to find specific files in "gopherspace." Currently, most teachers and students can find material on gopher servers using their Web browsers and more common search engines.

The ability to use Telnet to reach remote computers can be very useful for accessing information that has not yet become available through Web pages. Most Web browsers can summon programs such as NCSA Telnet and WinTel when the address for a Telnet site is entered. The Telnet program allows the user's computer to emulate a computer terminal connected to that remote host. So when searching a library catalog, for example, the user employs the catalog's specific commands. This can be confusing unless the user takes the time to read the help menus and onscreen prompts. A variety of Internet sources of value to schools, including academic and public library catalogs and systems, free-nets and community bulletin boards, and searchable databases, can be accessed through Telnet.

> **Not all Internet service providers carry all newsgroups, and the length of time a message remains available on a news server can vary.**

VI Obtaining, Uncompressing, and Using Files

SELF-ASSESSMENT

LEVEL 1   I cannot retrieve files from remote computers.

LEVEL 2   I know documents and computer programs that are useful to me and my students are stored on computers throughout the world. I cannot retrieve these files.

LEVEL 3   I understand the concept and netiquette of "anonymous" FTP sites. I can transfer files and programs from remote locations to my computer and can use programs or plug-ins that help me do this. I can extract compressed files and know some utilities that help me view graphics and play sounds and movies. I understand the nature and danger of computer viruses and know how to minimize my risk of contracting a computer virus.

LEVEL 4   I use information I have retrieved as a resource for and with my students. I understand the concept of a network server and the functions it can serve in an organization. I can use an FTP client to upload files to a server.

CLASS OBJECTIVES: OBTAINING, UNCOMPRESSING, AND USING FILES (3 HOURS)

1 Locate at least three reliable sites of freeware applications and documents. Know the difference between binary files and ASCII text files. Understand what makes a site reliable.

2 Use a search tool to locate a specific software application. Be able to determine how large the file is and how long it will take to download the file. Set a folder into which your files will be downloaded by using the Preferences setting in your browser.

3 Understand the meanings of the extensions .txt, .bin, .zip, .hqx, and .sit. Use Stuffit or Winzip to extract a compressed file. Know what files can be deleted after the decompression.

4 Know how to obtain and run a virus protection program.

5 Download a text file, graphic file, sound file, and program file.

6 Use an FTP program to upload a file to a server.

YOUR PORTFOLIO MIGHT INCLUDE:

1. a disk with a downloaded graphic, sound, movie, and program, each obtained from a remote host

2. the URLs from three *reliable* FTP sites on the Web

3. a written explanation of the concepts of freeware, shareware, and commercial software

WHY TEACHERS NEED TO KNOW HOW TO OBTAIN, UNCOMPRESS, AND USE FILES FROM REMOTE COMPUTERS

A very simplistic description of the purpose of any computer network is to move data from one storage device to another storage device electronically—usually over wires.

Increasingly, the processes computers and networks use to do this are fading into the background, becoming transparent to the user. Many of the deliberate, multistep, and command-laden procedures demanded by text-only mainframe accounts are being replaced by single-step, point-and-click actions. While more than a few "geeks" mourn the passing of commands such as FTP.SUNET.SE>get linc111.txt, for the vast majority of us, this has been a blessing.

The World Wide Web has absorbed many sites once created exclusively to store and make available files to remote users. These FTP (File Transfer Protocol) sites were a primary reason for the Internet's early existence—they enabled researcher A in New York to share her finding with Researcher B in Texas and Researcher C in California. Files the creators decided to make available to anyone could be put in folders that allowed "anonymous" log-on access;

FREE ADVICE: *If you have a shell account on a mainframe computer, you will need to first FTP the file to your host computer and then use a program such as Kermit to move it from the host to your desktop computer.*

When asked to log in to an "anonymous" FTP site, use your name as your user ID and your e-mail address as your password. It's the polite thing to do.

You may want to encourage your district to set up its own archive server of popular shareware, freeware, patches, and updates.

Storing and delivering computer software through networking is inexpensive for both the producers and the consumers. Eliminating cardboard boxes, floppy disks, shrink-wrap, warehouse space, postage, and remaindered copies can reduce the cost (and price) of software. And if this is true for software, would it not also hold true for music recordings, video recordings, and text?

HOMEWORK: Homework
Find and download the most recent version of a freeware virus protection program. Decompress and install it. Run it on the files on your computer's hard drive.

---

that was how freeware programmers made their latest versions available. These files are still available, but many text files have been converted to Web pages, and binary files of pictures or sound can be automatically viewed and played by helper applications within a Web browser. That primarily leaves binary files that are computer programs or patches that need to be treated in a special way.

Web browsers such as Netscape and Explorer make finding and downloading executable programs very simple. Websites such as **shareware.com <http://www.shareware.com/>, download.com <http://www.download.com/>, and filez <http://www.filez.com/>** contain most freeware and shareware programs or links to them. Click a hypertext link for the platform and version of the program you need, and the program is downloaded to a specified directory on your hard drive.

That's simple enough, but two additional steps need to be taken with most downloaded programs before they can be used. To conserve file space and decrease the amount of time it takes to move a file across the network, most programs are compressed (or stuffed or zipped), and once they are on the user's computer need to be decompressed (or unstuffed or unzipped) by a special utility. Most savvy users also use a utility to scan their new acquisitions for computer viruses. These ubiquitous bits of maliciously created code will destroy data and eat up file space if not found and destroyed.

The wealth of material available on the Internet for educators, however, makes learning these procedures worthwhile. Teachers can find:

▶ freeware, shareware, demonstration, and trial educational programs

▶ updates and patches to programs they already have

▶ the full text of many public-domain literary works and historical documents

▶ collections of clip art, fine art, photographs, movie clips, animations, and fonts

▶ commercial software that can be activated with a "key" once payment for it is made

VII | Real-Time and Push Technologies

SELF-ASSESSMENT

LEVEL 1   I use only static documents and files I retrieve from the Internet.

LEVEL 2   I have information sent to me on a regular basis through e-mail, and I check sites for information on a regular basis.

LEVEL 3   I use chatrooms and customized news and information feeds. I can listen to audio streamed from the Web. I know the hardware and software requirements for Web-based videoconferencing.

LEVEL 4   I can use real-time applications to design a virtual classroom or interactive learning experience. My students use videoconferencing for communication with experts and project collaboration with other students.

CLASS OBJECTIVES: REAL-TIME AND PUSH TECHNOLOGIES (3 HOURS)

1 Understand the difference and give examples of synchronous and asynchronous forms of communication. Know what is meant by "real time" communications.

2 Install and configure an Internet Relay Chat (IRC) client on your computer. Locate and log on to an IRC server. Read and respond to an ongoing chat. Quit from the session and exit the program.

3 Install and configure a client to receive streamed audio broadcasts. Locate a source of audio, either voice or music. Play a selection.

4 Install and configure the hardware (camera and microphone) and software needed to conduct a two-way videoconference. Connect with a remote site and conduct the conference. Understand the hardware, software, and network speed and bandwidth requirements for Internet videoconferencing.

5 Install a personalized news application such as PointCast or Educast. Select interest areas and update times.

YOUR PORTFOLIO MIGHT INCLUDE:

1. a list of Internet sources, including:
   - educational chatrooms
   - news and information pushed to the desktop
   - sites that provide music and speech broadcast through audio streaming
2. the results of an Internet videoconference, including a list of resources necessary and a commentary of the possible uses of the technology in education

➤ TEACHERS' NEED FOR REAL-TIME AND PUSH TECHNOLOGIES

The sender and receiver of a message in an asynchronous mode do not have to share common space in time to communicate. Asynchronous communication technologies include books, letters, audio and video recordings, e-mail, and voice mail. To communicate in a synchronous mode, the sender and receiver of the message must share common space in time. Examples of synchronous communication technologies are plays and readings, telephone calls, videoconferences, live audio and video broadcasts, and conversation.

The Internet has always been a means for teachers and students to communicate asynchronously. Accessing Web pages of text and graphics, downloading files, and reading e-mail do not require the sender and the receiver of the message to be communicating at the same time. But some Internet technologies are "real-time," synchronous forms of communication.

One of the oldest and most common real-time Internet communications modes is Internet Relay Chat. A teacher or student using a special program

---

FREE ADVICE: *Neal Stephenson's science fiction novel* Snowcrash *uses a highly sophisticated virtual world populated by digital representations of humans called "avatars." The book is a fascinating read for those who might like a glimpse of what the next generation of chatrooms might look like.*

Why pay for long distance phone calls when you can use your computer and your Internet connection instead of the telephone company's switched services? At the present time, Internet telephony requires common software on both parties' computers and a tolerance for poor sound quality. But the blending of your computer and telephone seems inevitable.

Another example of push technology is being used by the online bookstore Amazon.com, <http://www.Amazon.com>. Tell Amazon your favorite author or topic of interest, and it will send you e-mail to let you know when new titles are published that meet your specifications.

 HOMEWORK: Download and install the Educast software. Configure the program to your specification.

Download and install RealAudio software. Make sure the plug-in for your browser is installed. Find a newscast to share with your class.

---

such as IRCle or Talk can join a typed conversation in a virtual room, listening and adding to the ongoing conversation. Like the content of newsgroups, the topics and value of chatrooms vary widely but can be used for interesting educational purposes, especially if the chat is arranged for a specific purpose at an agreed-upon time with known participants. Teachers also need some knowledge of chatrooms simply to understand their attraction to many of their students.

Real Audio **<http://www.real.com>** is a tool that allows the user to listen to music and voice in a broadcast fashion. Through a method called "streaming," the sound file is played as it is being sent across the network, allowing very long selections to be heard at a surprisingly high quality. News, feature programs, sports, music, and historical recordings all can be found and used in the classroom.

As schools obtain faster networks with greater bandwidth, they are beginning to use the Internet for videoconferencing. Video cameras not much larger than a golf ball are available for less than $100. Along with shareware such as CU-SeeMe, they allow teachers and students not just to hear experts and collaborators from around the world but to see them and share a common whiteboard for text and diagrams. For the time being, the quality is low and the connections are difficult to establish, but it is a lively use of networks even if done within a building or district. Videoconferencing has the possibility of becoming a serious business use for networks.

Do you not only want to read the news that is important to you but be able to do so as soon as it happens? "Push" technologies used by programs such as PointCast **<http://www.pointcast.com>** and Educast **<http://www.educast.com>** make that possible. After installing the software, the user selects what topics, news sources, and locales to have pushed to his or her computer, and how often. For a teacher with a direct network connection, this means having an up-to-the-minute, customized newspaper waiting on the classroom computer for use with the class.

VIII Web Page Construction

SELF-ASSESSMENT

LEVEL 1   I cannot create a page that can be viewed with a Web browser.

LEVEL 2   I can save text I've created as an HTML file with a command in my word processor. I know a few, simple HTML commands.

LEVEL 3   Using hand-coded HTML or a Web page authoring tool, I can:

▶ view Web pages as a source documents

▶ create a formatted Web page that uses background color, font styles and alignment, graphics, and tables

▶ include links to other parts of my document or other Internet sites in my page

▶ understand basic guidelines for good Web page construction and the district's Web policies

LEVEL 4   I can use the Web as an interface to databases. When appropriate, I can register my pages with search engine sites. I can help write Web creation policies for design, content, and use.

CLASS OBJECTIVES: WEB PAGE CONSTRUCTION (3 HOURS):

1 Know the terms HTML, tags, hypertext, and links.

2 Use a text processor to create an original Web page that has the HTML tags for:

■ a head, title, body, and footer
■ line breaks, paragraph breaks, horizontal rules, and size headings
■ the text styles bold, underline, and italic
■ numbered and bulleted lists
■ a link to another Web page
■ insertion and alignment of a graphic

3 Save the file with an HTM or HTML extention.

4 Know when to use direct HTML tags and when to use logical HTML tags.

5 Use an HTML program such as Microsoft Frontpage, Claris Homepage, or Netscape Composer to:

■ import the text page created above
■ add a background color
■ add information to a table
■ add internal links within the document
■ create a graphic that is a hypertext link

6 Know Web page construction guidelines that make pages useable for a range of browsers and friendly to users with slower Internet connections.

7 Understand the procedures for uploading pages to the school's Web server. Know the school's Web server and Web page construction guidelines.

YOUR PORTFOLIO MIGHT INCLUDE:

1. a printout of the source for an original HTML page and the page itself on a disk. The page must include:

■ background color
■ font styles
■ a graphic
■ links to related sources

2. a copy of the district's Web page guidelines

TEACHERS' NEED FOR A BASIC UNDERSTANDING OF WEB PAGE CONSTRUCTION

Most of the skills this chapter has suggested have been to help teachers access information from the Internet. Increasingly, however, teachers, students, and schools are using the Web to publish a variety of informational resources for the community, including:

▶ staff directories

▶ events calendars that can be maintained by individual departments or schools

▶ searchable library catalogs and curriculum resource databases

▶ uniform, accessible, and modifiable curricula

▶ news of class activities and events for parents

▶ surveys, questionnaires, and guest books

▶ lunch menus

▶ new resident information about registration and maps of attendance areas

> The ability to help students publish the results of their research, creative writings, and other classroom projects is perhaps the most exciting way teachers can use the Internet

FREE ADVICE: *Many word processors now allow the user to save a document as HTML. These are surprisingly good at creating a simple page or a page that can be easily enhanced with a dedicated Web page program.*

Districts need good Web page and Web site guidelines that address such issues as the educational purpose of the Web server, the responsibilities for its upkeep, and the content, style, and mechanical requirements of original Web pages. Guidelines should also specify permissions needed and allowable personal information that can be included on student pages. Mankato's guidelines can be found at **http://www.isd77.k12.mn.us/ webguide.HTML.**

Remember that Web pages need to be updated and maintained. Don't start Web pages that will quickly become "cobweb" pages.

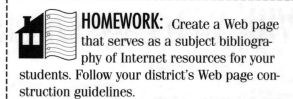

HOMEWORK: Create a Web page that serves as a subject bibliography of Internet resources for your students. Follow your district's Web page construction guidelines.

Teachers can also use originally authored Web pages to replace or supplement paper handouts for their classes. The pages might include:

▶ information about the class content, assignments, and expectations

▶ criteria for class projects and self-assessment tools

▶ online tutorials and guides

▶ bibliographies of print and electronic resources

▶ links to class bulletin boards for virtual discussions

▶ addresses of experts and mentors willing to work with students

For the truly adventurous teacher, there exists the possibility of creating entire classes that are taught and taken online. These classes can be offered throughout the world to anyone with an Internet connection. Commercial sources of such coursework as DigitalThink <http://www.digital-think.com> and a variety of virtual high schools are early models of effective online education.

The ability to help students publish the results of their research, creative writings, and other classroom projects is perhaps the most exciting way teachers can use the Internet and the best reason they need to know how to create original Web pages. Writing experts have known for a long time that all writers take more care with their writing when they know it will be published for a wide audience. The Internet is a fine place for publishing student work and can serve as an excellent source of practice assessment materials for preservice teachers.

Ⅸ Learning Opportunities Using the Internet

SELF-ASSESSMENT

LEVEL 1   I am not aware of any ways the Internet can be used with students in my classroom.

LEVEL 2   I occasionally allow my students to use the Internet to find information.

LEVEL 3   I know a variety of projects and activities that effectively use the Internet to instruct and involve students. I know a source for collaborative projects, can direct students to online tutorials and learning resources, and encourage a variety of keypal activities.

LEVEL 4   I can design and implement an Internet project or maintain an educational Internet site.

 ## CLASS OBJECTIVES: LEARNING OPPORTUNITIES USING THE INTERNET (3 HOURS)

1 Identify and categorize student uses of the Internet, including:

- keypal projects
- collaborative writing projects
- access to experts
- primary source data gathering using surveys
- secondary source gathering
- virtual field trips
- participation in interactive projects
- publication of student work on the Web

2 Locate print and online sources of student projects, activities, and resources.

3 Know characteristics of an Internet project that will increase its likelihood of success.

4 Find three areas in your curriculum that could be supplemented by the use of Internet resources or activities. Include assessments that are specific to Internet use.

 ## YOUR PORTFOLIO MIGHT INCLUDE:

a list of three classroom activities that use Web resources, including at least one that is interactive in nature and one that requires collaboration with students in another school

TEACHERS' NEED TO KNOW LEARNING OPPORTUNITIES USING THE INTERNET

One happy way the Internet distinguishes itself from other educational technologies is that it can be truly interactive. No longer does the use of technology need to be associated with students' passive absorption of information projected, played, or broadcast. The Internet, when used well, asks students to be creators and senders, as well as receivers, of information.

Some of the ways teachers have successfully used technology with students include:

▶ **KEYPAL PROJECTS.** Students or groups of students communicate with other students at a remote location, whether across town or across the world. Increased understanding of language, a better knowledge of another culture, and more motivation for writing are common results. A variety of Internet sites help teachers find and successfully use keypals.

▶ **COLLABORATIVE WRITING PROJECTS.** Student writing can easily be shared with others across the Internet. Other readers can comment, edit, revise, or add to the student work, which can then be returned. And it's a great learning experience for students to edit and revise the writing of others.

▶ **ACCESS TO EXPERTS AND MENTORS.** Physical visits by authors, scientists, political figures, athletes,

 FREE ADVICE: *These books are among the best at suggesting strategies and student uses of the Internet in the curriculum:*

■ *Harris,* Way of the Ferret: Finding and Using Educational Resources on the Internet. 2nd ed. *ISTE, 1995*

■ *Roerden,* Net Lessons: Web-Based Projects for Your Classroom, *O'Reilly, 1997*

■ *Simpson and McElmeel,* Internet for Schools. 2nd ed. *Linworth, 1997*

■ *Williams,* The Internet for Teachers. 2nd ed. *IDG, 1996*

Most teachers did not use the Internet as a source of information and activities in their own formal education. The Internet itself has not always proven to be a fast or reliable educational resource. And a good deal of what is accessible using the Internet has little value in education. For these reasons and probably others, it is unlikely your first classroom experience with the Internet will be successful. Accept that, and try a variety of strategies. Our students need the practice in using this valuable resource.

 HOMEWORK: Access the Global Schoolhouse Network **<http://www.gsn.org/>** and identify a project that supports your curriculum. Subscribe to the HILITES mailing list of student projects.

and other subject specialists are often impossible for schools to arrange. Virtual visits through e-mail, chatrooms, or videoconferencing are less expensive and less time consuming for the visitor and can be just as meaningful.

▶ **PRIMARY SOURCE DATA GATHERING USING SURVEYS.** Many student projects involve using the Internet to gather and compile data. Classrooms collect information from other schools throughout the country and the world about topics as diverse as the weather, holiday customs, and pollution indicators. A wonderful site that helps facilitate these projects is educational technology pioneer Al Rogers' Global Schoolhouse Network **<http://www.gsn.org/>**.

▶ **SECONDARY SOURCE GATHERING.** Perhaps the first, and least threatening way teachers can use the Internet as a part of their curriculum is by encouraging students to use Internet-based information to complete research projects. Teachers first need to learn and help teach their students the skills in Rubric IV, Search Tools.

▶ **VIRTUAL FIELD TRIPS.** Many organizations are putting a virtual version of themselves on the Internet. The ability to view the contents of museums, actual and recreated historical sites, research labs, and even other countries has removed the barrier of distance from field trips. As virtual technologies improve from the now primitive digital movies and VRML, this will become an increasingly useful and exciting means of using the Internet.

▶ **PARTICIPATION IN FORMAL INTERACTIVE PROJECTS.** A variety of organizations and companies sponsor nationwide projects for students. The Journey North, MayaQuest, and Geogame are among the more popular projects that are well organized and have strong educational goals.

▶ **PUBLICATION OF STUDENT WORK ON THE WEB.** The last section on Web publishing suggested that student work be displayed on the Internet for comment and review. One variation of sharing student work is to connect a video camera to the Internet so parents and others can view student performances such as speeches, readings, verbal reports, dramatizations, interviews, panel discussions, and debates. Students are more prepared and excited knowing there will be an audience beyond the classroom.

X Netiquette, Online Ethics, and Current Issues Surrounding Internet Use in K-12 Schools

SELF-ASSESSMENT

LEVEL 1   I am not aware of any ethics or proprieties regarding the Internet, nor am I aware of any issues dealing with Internet use in a school setting.

LEVEL 2   I understand a few rules my students and I should follow when using the Internet. I understand that the Internet is sometimes a controversial resource, which many educators and parents do not understand.

LEVEL 3   I have read a guideline for Internet use such as Arlene Rinaldi's *The Net: User Guidelines and Netiquette* and follow the rules outlined. I know and read the FAQ files associated with sources on the Internet. I am aware that electronic communication is a new communications medium that may require new sensitivities. I can identify print and online resources that speak to current Internet issues such as:

▶ censorship/site blocking software

▶ copyright

▶ legal and illegal uses

▶ data privacy

▶ security

I can list some of the critical components of a good acceptable use policy and know and use our district's policy.

LEVEL 4   I can use my knowledge of the Internet to write good school policies and activities that help students develop good judgment and good information skills.

CLASS OUTCOMES

This information and these skills are best taught as part of the training sessions to which they can be immediately applied.

Obtaining, Uncompressing, and Using Files from FTP Sites

1 Understand legal and illegal uses of software.

2 Understand how computer viruses are contracted, avoided, and eliminated.

3 Understand copyright issues regarding clip art, fonts, and other materials obtained from the Internet.

E-mail

4 Understand the basics of Internet netiquette.

World Wide Web Use and Web Page Construction

5 Know the district's acceptable use policy for network and Internet use.

6 Understand ethical and unethical uses of school equipment.

7 Know how data can be secured and privacy protected.

8 Know any Web page construction guidelines.

YOUR PORTFOLIO MIGHT INCLUDE:

1. a word processed statement no longer than two pages containing:
   - ■ your personal philosophy of the use of the Internet in education
   - ■ a definition and example of freeware, shareware, and commercial software
2. a copy of the district's Internet and copyright policies

► TEACHERS' NEED FOR UNDERSTANDING ONLINE ETHICS

Why do technology ethics deserve special attention? There are a variety of reasons:

► Using technology to communicate and operate in a "virtual world," one that only exists within computers and computer networks, is a new phenomenon that is not always well understood by teachers who received their primary education prior to its existence.

► Our new technological capabilities may require new ethical considerations.

■ The ability to send unsolicited commercial messages to millions of Internet e-mail users (spamming) was not possible before there was e-mail or the Internet.

■ Digital photography has made the manipulation of images undetectable, a feat impossible with chemical photography.

■ Prior to the Internet, minors faced physical barriers of access to sexually explicit materials.

 FREE ADVICE: *Distribute copies of your district's acceptable use policy, copyright policies, Web use guidelines, and other relevant documents during the first training session and ask that they be included in all student portfolios.*

While an entire school or district may wish to use a single set of guidelines, each classroom teacher needs to understand, teach, and model the guidelines. Simple, easily remembered guidelines for children are probably the best.

Johnson's Three Ps of Technology Ethics:

1 *Privacy—I will protect my privacy and respect the privacy of others.*

2 *Property—I will protect my property and respect the property of others.*

3 *a(P)propriate use—I will use technology in constructive ways and in ways that do not break the rules of my family, church, school, or government.*

Keep parents informed about how the Internet is being used in your school and classroom. Stories in the media often portray the Internet as a frightening place. Parents and the community need to know that teachers understand the dangers and limitations of the Internet and are using it in constructive, important ways.

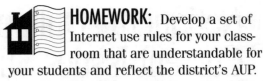 **HOMEWORK:** Develop a set of Internet use rules for your classroom that are understandable for your students and reflect the district's AUP. Read Rinaldi's netiquette guide <http://www.fau.edu:80/rinaldi/net/index.HTM>.

■ Intellectual property in digital format can now be duplicated with incredible ease.

► There is a temptation to view one's actions in the intangible, virtual world of information technologies as being less serious than one's actions in the real world. Information technology misuse by many people, especially the young, is viewed as a low-risk, game-like challenge.

Not long ago, ethical technology questions were only of interest to a very few specialists. But as the use of information technologies spreads throughout society and its importance to our national economies and individual careers grows, everyone will need to make good ethical decisions when using computers. Studies show that persons involved in computer crimes acquire both their interest and their skills at an early age.

Teachers need to know the ethical issues of technology and be able to conduct informed discussions with students as a part of regular technology training and when technology misuse occurs. Perhaps even more importantly, teachers need to demonstrate the ethical use of technologies. Effective monitoring of student activities cannot occur unless the teacher knows of possible actions that are ethically and legally improper.

Applied ethics needs to be an integral part of technology use in schools. Technology, especially electronic communications, has proven to be a tempting medium for new types of mischief, vandalism, and other more serious crimes. Early education about the ethical use of technologies may help stem the abuse of those technologies as students grow older.

Students need the chance to discuss how technology will impact the society and culture in which they live. Concepts of privacy, property, and appropriateness are often difficult for teachers to approach since the values inherent in them can be interpreted quite differently—even within a single school system, depending on its families' religious and political beliefs. This difficulty must not be used as an excuse to avoid such issues. One responsible approach is to deal with ethical issues in the context of civics instruction.

CHAPTER 4

Rubics for Restructuring: Advanced CODE 77 Rubics

 The only way to discover the limits of the possible is to go beyond them into the impossible.
—Arthur C. Clarke

The computer skills we have examined so far—basic computer operation, word processing, telecommunication, record keeping, and Internet use—help teachers improve their professional productivity. But if technology is to realize its powerful potential for radically improving education, it must be used for more than just automating the traditional methods and practices of teaching.

The rubrics below are designed to help teachers move to a higher level of professional computer use. Rather than using the computer simply as a tool that allows a common task to be done more efficiently, these skills modify how instruction is delivered, how student performance is measured, and how teachers view themselves as professionals. The technology is

used to restructure the educational process to assure that:

▶ all students master the basic skills of writing, reading, and computation

▶ all students practice information literacy and research skills, and the higher order thinking skills inherent in them

▶ all teachers have the tools and ability

   ■ to locate the research findings that will guide their professional practice

   ■ to collect the data that measure the effectiveness of their methodologies

These advanced rubrics are designed for the same purposes as the beginning CODE 77 rubrics and the Internet rubrics: to help schools measure the effectiveness of their teacher training efforts and to help guide teachers on their own learning paths.

How does one design training to help teachers master these complex skills? Developing and practicing these competencies will be a far greater, more time-consuming task than the simple hands-on classes in which word processing, e-mail, and file management are taught. And the technology department alone can't do it. Staff development in these technology uses will require collaborative efforts with specialists in content areas, child development, curriculum, assessment, research, and evaluation. It will also require a team comprising the teacher, principal, staff development coordinator, and media specialist or technology coordinator to devise an individualized, long-range development plan for each teacher.

> After mastering the necessary basic skills in the preceding chapters, a teacher or group of teachers should pick one or two advanced rubrics on which to work each year.

Because of the long-range nature of these staff development efforts, sample professional growth plans, rather than a list of specific skills taught in classes, are described for each rubric. After mastering the necessary basic skills in the preceding chapters, a teacher or group of teachers should pick one or two advanced rubrics on which to work each year. The teachers' supervisor or staff development leader can then evaluate the completion of the professional growth plan as district policy requires.

These challenging skills will take time, effort, and courage to master, but schools with teachers who do so will be in a superior position to meet future educational demands.

⬛I Instructional Software Use

SELF-ASSESSMENT

LEVEL 1   I do not use instructional software as a part of my instructional program, nor am I aware of any titles that might help my students meet their learning goals.

LEVEL 2   I use a few computer programs as an instructional supplement, as a reward, or with special needs children.

LEVEL 3   I use several programs chosen by my department or grade level, such as drill and practice, simulations, and tutorials, to help all my students meet specific learning objectives. The software allows me to teach and reinforce concepts more effectively than traditional methods. When it is available, I use the software's management system to help assess individual student performance. I use the school's integrated learning system in a purposeful way.

LEVEL 4   I seek out new programs for evaluation and adoption. I know sources of software reviews and keep current on developments in computer technologies through professional reading and conference attendance. I share my findings with other professionals.

PROFESSIONAL GROWTH PLAN TO MEET THIS COMPETENCY

The professional growth plan is to be written in collaboration with the curriculum director or department chair and technology coordinator or media specialist.

1 I will examine my curriculum to determine two areas in which the use of technology may help improve student acquisition of knowledge, concepts, or skills. The learning goals for these areas will be clearly articulated.

2 I will review the professional literature for my subject area for recommended software titles and methods for using the software. I will attend a technology conference and attend sessions appropriate to software use in my area and visit software vendor displays.

3 I will personally conduct a hands-on review of selected software titles. (Preview copies may need to be purchased, cataloged, and placed in the district or school software preview library.)

4 I will incorporate the use of selected software titles into my lessons, recording through testing or observation the effectiveness and appropriateness of the software.

5 I will report the results of the use of the selected titles to the appropriate curriculum committee and recommend whether the district should adopt the software or not. I will share my findings through in-district workshops or on staff development days.

6 (Optional) I will take a college class, seminar, or workshop on the use of instructional software in the classroom.

YOUR PORTFOLIO MIGHT INCLUDE:

1. a copy of your department's resource guide with computer software applications noted

2. copies of at least three lesson plans that incorporate the use of the software

3. original reviews of three pieces of subject-specific computer software that support the district curriculum

4. short observations on the efficacy of the software in the instructional process

5. a plan to use an integrated learning system with individual students

WHY TEACHERS NEED INSTRUCTIONAL SOFTWARE USE SKILLS

The public has a less-than stellar-view of education's performance. Routinely, public schools are lambasted for everything from poor test scores to high dropout rates to rising costs. Yet the professionals who staff schools are, by and large, competent, caring, well educated, and dedicated. What's going on?

Perhaps we need to ask not why schools are less effective than they once were, but why they aren't as good as they need to be. Studies show that our national economy has changed. In 1950, fully 65% of our students could leave school, with or without a diploma, and obtain gainful employment that paid a living wage. By the year 2000, less than 15% of our workers will be employed in nonskilled jobs. The automation of industry and the use of low-paid foreign labor markets have resulted in an economy in which all workers must have excellent basic skills and increasingly sophisticated levels of problem-solving, creative-thinking, communication, and interpersonal skills in order to have jobs that provide a decent standard of living. And yet the "raw product" coming into our schools has not changed much since the 1950s. Homes of poverty, substance abuse, violence, and neglect still exist, and the distractions of jobs, television, and video games seem to draw children away from the brain-building activities of studying, reading, drawing, and conversation.

Schools are finding that society is demanding we educate an increasingly less educable population. This helps explain why using expensive, fickle computer software is preferable to using traditional methods of instruction under certain conditions. Electronic resources have proven useful when:

▶ **A LESSON CAN BE TAUGHT MORE EASILY, QUICKLY, OR EFFECTIVELY.** Students who may not be able to master basic skills from lectures, workbooks, or texts can and do learn them from the highly interactive, self-paced instruction offered by integrated learning systems.

▶ **THE TIMELINESS OF THE LESSON'S CONTENT IS ESSENTIAL.** We know most students respond best when the information or skills have relevance to their lives. Examples, problems, and readings from the students' world are easily accessible with information technologies like the Internet.

▶ **MOTIVATION IS NECESSARY.** The immediate feedback, interesting graphics, and amusing sounds designed into many computer programs can make learning more enticing to many children accustomed to video games and television. It's true we use computers too often as electronic flash cards, but for some educational purposes flash cards are just what is needed.

▶ **A LEARNING OPPORTUNITY CANNOT BE OFFERED BY OTHER MEANS.** Experiencing a ride through the human body, building and administering a city, and seeing a geometry theorem through animation can only be done with technology.

▶ **THE SKILL BEING TAUGHT IS A REAL-WORLD TECHNICAL SKILL.** Employers expect our graduates to come into the workplace knowing how to use technology to communicate, calculate, and access information. The same types of productivity software used in business are needed in schools.

Teachers have always had to meet a variety of educational goals: teaching for both facts and concept attainment, developing both lower- and higher-level thinking skills, and increasing both knowledge about and positive attitudes toward a subject. The tools with which they have had to work have not changed much in the past hundred years. But now judiciously used computer software can help teachers reach all these educational objectives with all students—just as our parents, communities, and nation are asking us to do.

> Employers expect our graduates to come into the workplace knowing how to use technology to communicate, calculate, and access information.

II Using Technology to Improve Student Writing

PROFESSIONAL GROWTH PLAN TO MEET THIS COMPETENCY

The professional growth plan is to be written in collaboration with the department chair or district writing team and technology coordinator or media specialist.

1 I will examine my curriculum to determine two uses of technology that may help my students improve their writing. The objectives for these uses will be clearly articulated.

2 I will review the professional literature about best practices in teaching writing, looking especially for recommended hardware, software titles, and teaching techniques. I will attend a technology conference and attend sessions appropriate to writing and visit software vendor displays.

3 I will personally give a hands-on review of selected writing software titles. (Preview copies may need to be purchased and then cataloged and placed in the district or school software preview library.)

4 I will incorporate the use of selected writing software or hardware into my lessons, recording through testing and observation the effectiveness and appropriateness of the software.

5 I will report the results of the use of the selected titles and techniques to the appropriate curriculum committee, and recommend whether the district should adopt the software and techniques. I will share my findings through in-district workshops or on staff development days.

6 (Optional) I will take a college class, seminar, or workshop on the use of technology in teaching writing.

YOUR PORTFOLIO MIGHT INCLUDE:

1. descriptions of technology and techniques used in your classroom to help students improve their writing

2. assessments used with these tools

3. a copy of the district's writing curriculum with modifications and recommendations for using technology

4. personal journal reflections on using technology in the writing process, including what does and does not work well

WHY TEACHERS NEED SKILLS IN USING TECHNOLOGY TO IMPROVE STUDENT WRITING

Among the most difficult but important communication abilities teachers can help students develop are writing skills. Effective communication of ideas through writing is essential, whether the product is a résumé, an advertisement, a bid, a short story, a college term paper, an editorial, or a love letter.

Computer technologies can help nearly every student become a more effective writer. Most teachers are by now familiar with word processors, those wonderful programs that allow writers to easily edit, print, and save their work. However, much software and hardware has been developed to help student writers during every phase of the writing process.

► **STORY STARTERS, TEMPLATES, AND IDEA GENERATORS.** Many word processors and writing packages include tools for getting reluctant writers started on the writing process by suggesting writing styles, characters, and situations.

► **PORTABLE WRITING COMPUTERS.** These inexpensive, battery-operated, book-sized devices allow students to compose and input text that can later be uploaded to a desktop computer for formatting and printing.

► **OUTLINERS AND ORGANIZERS.** In most word processors, writers can organize their ideas and information in an easily expandable and collapsible outline that can be transposed into regular text.

> Our poor writers can use the power of technology to become competent writers, and our good writers can use the tools to become terrific ones.

► **COMPUTERIZED THESAURI, SPELLING CHECKERS, AND GRAMMAR AIDES.** Misspellings, overused words, and suspect grammar and usage all can be detected with online tools that remove the communication difficulties caused by poor mechanics.

► **ONLINE COMMENT TOOLS.** A networked lab with the proper management system will allow students to electronically submit their writing for peer and teacher review.

► **FORMATTING TOOLS.** The ability to add headers and footers, columns, footnotes, a variety of font sizes and styles, bulleted and numbered lists, and tables can all vastly improve a writing's readability when properly used.

► **GRAPHIC AND DESKTOP PUBLISHING TOOLS.** Clip art, photographs, charts and graphs, text-boxes, and other visual images can help a student convey information and increase interest in a document. Simple student-produced newspapers can easily be created.

► **PUBLISHING TOOLS:** Printing student work is rapidly being supplemented by using the Web pages and e-mail to disseminate student writing for review and comment. Research shows that students write more carefully when they know their work will have a wide audience.

A computer will never write a poem or editorial any more than a telescope will ever discover a new galaxy. Yet our poor writers can use the power of technology to become competent writers, and our good writers can use the tools to become terrific ones. Teachers need both a strong conceptual background in process writing and an understanding of how technology can be used to enhance that process.

FREE ADVICE: *Students need to use spelling and grammar checkers as guides offering suggestions, not as authorities. These online tools can be incorrect.*

The play components of some children's writing and publishing tools can overshadow their educational purpose. Fancy fonts, animated graphics, and funny sounds may engender interest in a program, but rarely do they improve actual writing.

III Information Literacy Skills Using Secondary Sources

PROFESSIONAL GROWTH PLAN TO MEET THIS COMPETENCY

The growth plan is to be written in collaboration with the curriculum director or department chair and technology coordinator or media specialist.

1 I will obtain the district's information literacy curriculum, library and technology student benchmarks, assessment tools, and activity suggestions. (If these items do not exist, an alternate professional growth plan would describe how a teacher could help develop them.) I will examine my curriculum to determine if prescribed projects or lessons exist that teach information literacy skills.

2 I will review the literature for current descriptions of information literacy, especially as it applies to information technologies and digital information sources like the Internet.

3 I will plan and teach two projects that have information literacy/technology skills.

4 I will assess student work on these projects using tools that determine whether individuals met the benchmarked level of performance and use the findings as part of the student's grade, portfolio, or progress report.

5 I will examine the performance data for my classes and aggregate them to determine the efficacy of the activities and instruction and the validity of the benchmarks. I will share my findings through in-district workshops or on staff development days.

6 (Optional) I will take a college class, seminar, or workshop in information literacy or electronic research methods.

YOUR PORTFOLIO MIGHT INCLUDE:

1. descriptions of units taught in your classroom that have information literacy objectives as well as content objectives

2. assessment tools to use with students on these projects

3. a copy of the district's information literacy curriculum and student performance benchmarks in technology/information literacy

4. personal journal reflections on teaching information literacy skills, including what does and does not work well

⟩ WHY TEACHERS NEED AN INFORMATION LITERACY TECHNOLOGY SKILL SET USING SECONDARY SOURCES

The rapid growth of information in the past 50 years has placed an increased emphasis on the ability to find and use information, rather than simply memorize it. And while most school curricula have included library and research skills, changes in technology and educational philosophy have radically changed the skills scope and purpose:

▶ **PROCESS MODEL OF INFORMATION LITERACY.** Rather than students learning isolated skills on which they are given a test, best practice shows that library, computer, and research skills need to be combined

---

 FREE ADVICE: *A Research Question Rubric: Not all research questions are created equal.*

LEVEL ONE: *My research is about a broad topic. I can complete the assignment by using a general reference source such as an encyclopedia. I have no personal questions about the topic.* Example: My research is about the economy of Minnesota.

LEVEL TWO: *My research answers a question that helps me narrow the focus of my search. This question may mean that I need to go to various sources to gather enough information to get a reliable answer. The conclusion of the research will ask me to give a supported answer to the question.* Example: What role has manufacturing played in Minnesota's economic development?

LEVEL THREE: *My research answers a question of personal relevance. To answer this question, I may need to not just consult secondary sources such as magazines, newspapers, books, or the Internet, but to use primary sources of information such as original surveys, interviews, and source documents.* Example: How can one best prepare for a career in manufacturing in the Twin Cities area?

LEVEL FOUR: *My research answers a personal question about the topic and contains information that may be of use to decision-makers as they make policy or distribute funds. The result of my research is a well-supported conclusion that contains a call for action on the part of an organization or government body. There will be a plan to distribute this information.* Example: How might high schools change their curricula to meet the needs of students who want a career in manufacturing in Minnesota?

---

and taught as an applied process. A variety of such information on problem-solving process models exists, including Eisenberg and Berkowitz's "Big Six" approach. (*Information Problem-Solving.* Ablex, 1990.) Most models ask the researcher to:

- identify the research problem or question and determine the information needed to solve it
- determine possible sources of the needed information
- locate relevant information within the sources
- extract, record, and cite the information
- synthesize, evaluate, organize, and communicate or use the information
- evaluate the outcome and process

▶ **INTEGRATION INTO THE CLASSROOM.** The research process is moving away from being taught only in the media center or English classroom. The responsibility for students' becoming information literate is schoolwide and taught in all subject areas, as well as in multidisciplinary units. A teaching partnership with a qualified school media specialist is essential.

▶ **SHIFT IN ROLE OF THE TEACHER FROM INFORMATION PROVIDER TO FACILITATOR.** Many teachers recognize that by helping students find, evaluate, analyze, and use information they become even more important than they were as lecturers.

▶ **ELECTRONIC RESOURCES.** The printed encyclopedia and magazine back issues are rapidly being replaced by their CD-ROM or online versions, which are more comprehensive, timely, and easily searched. Internet access to remote library catalogs and the World Wide Web have vastly expanded the resources available to student researchers in even the smallest schools. The unregulated, unedited nature of the Internet is demanding an increased emphasis on teaching students how to evaluate the information they find.

▶ **ELECTRONIC COMMUNICATING DEVICES.** Just as information can be found through electronic means, the ability to communicate it using technology has also vastly increased. Word processed term papers, electronic slide presentations, hypermedia productions, and Web pages are all common methods of reporting the findings of research.

▶ **GENUINE QUESTIONING AND PROBLEM-SOLVING.** Using research to answer genuine questions of student interest and help solve real life problems promotes higher-order thinking and increases student interest in learning.

These changes have come about since most teachers have been in school themselves. For some, the shift from information provider to information guide will be a difficult one. But these are skills that will allow students to be the creative problem-solvers employers are demanding.

IV Information Literacy Skills Using Primary Sources

SELF-ASSESSMENT

LEVEL 1 When asking students to do research, I expect them to only use secondary resources like books, magazines, or reference materials.

LEVEL 2 As a part of my curriculum, I have some units that require the collection and use of original data. I generally can predict the outcome of such experiments.

LEVEL 3 My curriculum includes at least two information literacy projects that require the collection of original data to answer a genuine question. I may use tools to collect data, such as computerized probes and sensors, online surveys, interviews, and digitized sources of historical records, as well as tools to record, organize, and communicate the data, such as databases and spreadsheets.

LEVEL 4 I am actively involved in curriculum planning teams and advocate for multidisciplinary units and activities that require information literacy skills. I share successful units with others through print and electronic publishing and through conference presentations and workshops.

PROFESSIONAL GROWTH PLAN TO MEET THIS COMPETENCY

The growth plan is to be written in collaboration with the curriculum director or department chair and technology coordinator or media specialist.

1 I will obtain the district's information literacy curriculum, library and technology student benchmarks, assessment tools, and activity suggestions. (If these items do not exist, an alternate professional growth plan would describe how a teacher could help develop them.) I will examine my curriculum to determine the existence of prescribed projects or lessons that teach information literacy skills.

2 I will review the literature for current descriptions of information literacy, especially as it applies to using primary sources of information and data gathering techniques.

3 I will plan and teach two projects that have information literacy/technology skills and use primary source data to help answer the research question.

4 I will assess student work on these projects using tools that determine whether individuals met the benchmarked level of performance and use the findings as part of the student's grade, portfolio, or progress report.

5 I will examine the performance data for my classes and aggregate it to determine the efficacy of the activities and instruction and the validity of the benchmarks. I will share my findings through in-district workshops or on staff development days.

6 (Optional) I will take a college class, seminar, or workshop information literacy or research methods using primary data.

YOUR PORTFOLIO MUST INCLUDE:

1. descriptions of units taught in your classroom that have information literacy objectives and content objectives that include the use of primary sources

2. assessment tools to use with students on these projects

3. a copy of the district's information literacy curriculum and student performance benchmarks in technology /information literacy

4. personal journal reflections on teaching information literacy skills, including what does and does not work well

➤ WHY TEACHERS NEED AN INFORMATION LITERACY TECHNOLOGY SKILL SET USING PRIMARY SOURCES

Consider these actual research assignments:

▶ High school students trace the history of a building on their town's main street through interviews and courthouse records. They publish their findings in the local newspaper.

▶ Students in a technology education class use computerized timers to develop the most aerodynamically efficient design for a racecar.

▶ A middle school class learns about World War II by interviewing the town's senior citizens and creating Web pages of their stories, photographs, and memorabilia related to that time period.

▶ Elementary students collect holiday customs celebrated by students from around the world using electronic mail and the Internet.

▶ Students poll the community for their suggestions on how schools can be improved.

Increasingly common, projects like these have qualities that make them both effective and potentially frustrating:

1 THE RESEARCH FOCUSES ON TOPICS OF LOCAL SIGNIFICANCE. Whether researching a building, person, immigrant group, or custom, the emphasis is on things in the student's immediate geographic area, if not in his or her own household. Even when the topic is of national or international scope—pollution, the global economy, the Gulf War, technology, or health issues—teachers are asking students to assess the impact of policies and events on their own families and communities.

2 RESEARCHERS ARE BEING ASKED TO USE PRIMARY, RATHER THAN SECONDARY, SOURCES. Local history and current data are scanty in most school media centers, and when they do exist, perhaps in back issues of the local newspaper or in government documents, they are not often indexed

or are difficult to obtain. The county courthouse, a local university, original surveys, government statistics (published on the Internet), and the memories of local "experts" are examples of primary information sources in increasingly common use.

3 PROJECTS ARE PURPOSELY DESIGNED TO BE MEANINGFUL TO THE STUDENT RESEARCHER. The issues of World War II become exciting when told by the people who actually were affected by them. The genuine voices of another culture's students of a similar age speak louder than any text or reference book.

The tasks of the information process (see a description of the Big Six in the previous rubric) remain much the same regardless of the source of the information. Students still need to formulate good questions and identify the needed information. They still need a method of gathering, recording, organizing, and analyzing the information, whether those tasks are accomplished with paper and pencil, videocamera, database, or e-mail. However, primary data need to be critically evaluated even more skillfully than data gleaned from edited secondary information sources.

> The tasks of the information process remain much the same regardless of the source of the information.

As performance-based assessment becomes a standard means of evaluating student work, the communication of the researched findings becomes increasingly important. Students need guidance in deciding the medium and preparing the display of their findings, whether through thoughtfully crafted charts and graphs, multimedia presentations, computerized slide shows, or even Web pages.

For many teachers, who probably were not asked to do primary source research until they were in graduate school—if ever—the use of original research and primary sources may be as new as it is to their students. An educational philosophy that accepts knowledge growth and skill acquisition by both the student *and* the teacher is essential.

V Modification of Instructional Delivery

 PROFESSIONAL GROWTH PLAN TO MEET THIS COMPETENCY

The growth plan is to be written in collaboration with the instructional development or staff development coordinator.

1 I will review the professional literature to find examples of teaching and classroom management techniques that allow me to vary my instructional delivery strategies. These might include:

- individualized instruction using self-paced instructional software
- small-group task work with a computer assigned to each team
- technology-enhanced presentation techniques
- interactive video used to bring in outside experts or information resources
- online instruction using Web-based curricula, readings, bulletin boards, discussions, assessments, or telementoring

I will examine my curriculum to determine where such instruction might prove more effective than large-group lecturing.

2 I will use researched technology-aided instructional method during the school year, recording through testing and observation the effectiveness and appropriateness of the methodology.

3 I will report the results of the use of the method to the staff development committee and recommend whether the district should encourage its continued use through staff development classes. I will share my findings through in-district workshops or on staff development days.

4 (Optional) I will take a college class, seminar, or workshop on the use of technology-aided instructional methods.

 YOUR PORTFOLIO MIGHT INCLUDE:

1. lesson plans that use cooperative groups using technology to meet a learning objective

2. printouts of a self-made computer slide show, videotape, or URL for a Web site used to help teach a unit

3. descriptions and observations of online teaching, advising, or mentoring

➤ WHY TEACHERS NEED THE ABILITY TO USE TECHNOLOGY TO MODIFY INSTRUCTIONAL DELIVERY

Research on learning styles, multiple intelligences, and effective teaching practices suggests that not all teaching methods work well with all students under all circumstances. Technology can significantly increase the number of tools available to teachers, improving their teaching effectiveness with all learners. Individual instruction, small group instruction, and whole class instruction can all benefit from the thoughtful use of technology:

▶ Individualized instruction using self-paced software (either stand-alone titles or in an integrated learning system) can help students who need additional practice or a second or third approach to the material. Diagnostic modules can help determine and monitor student skill attainment.

▶ Small groups, with a computer assigned to each group, can use the technology as a tool for data recording and communication. Simulations, experiments, and research projects are also better accomplished through teamwork.

▶ Technology-enhanced presentations using slide shows or multimedia programs capture and

> Technology can significantly increase the number of tools available to teachers, improving their teaching effectiveness with all learners.

retain student interest and can enhance student understanding of concepts through visual representations like graphs, charts, and pictures. These programs also allow the teacher to rapidly update content. Student use of these programs should be encouraged as well.

▶ Internet-based collaborative projects allow students to interact with others throughout the world in meaningful ways. Key-pals, collaborative data gathering projects such as Journey North **<http://www.learner.org/jnorth/index.html>**, and virtual tours such as MayaQuest **<http://www. classroom.com/mayaquest/>** excite students with their immediacy and relevance.

▶ Interactive video can be used to bring in outside subject experts and provide virtual tours of museums, businesses, or organizations.

▶ Online instruction using Web-based curricula, readings, bulletin boards, discussions, assessments, and telementoring increases learning opportunities for students.

As the economy increasingly requires all workers to have high skill levels, the ability to teach all students effectively will become increasingly important. Teachers will need all the good pedagogical tools they can use.

VI Assessment of Student Performance

SELF-ASSESSMENT

LEVEL 1 I evaluate my students using objective tests only.

LEVEL 2 I evaluate some student performances or projects using subjective criteria. I save some student work for cumulative folders and parent conferences, and print some electronically produced student work.

LEVEL 3 I use a wide range of assessments to evaluate student projects and performances. I can use technology to create assessment tools like checklists, rubrics, and benchmarks that help the student assess his or her own performance and allow me to objectively determine the quality of student work. I ask students to keep both a physical and electronic portfolio of their work. I have a computerized means of aggregating performance data for my class that I use to modify my teaching activities and strategies.

LEVEL 4 I continuously try new approaches suggested by research or observation to discover the most effective means of using technology to help assess student learning. I work with a team of fellow teachers to create, modify, and improve my work in this area.

 ## PROFESSIONAL GROWTH PLAN TO MEET THIS COMPETENCY

The growth plan is to be completed with the district assessment director or committee.

1 I will review the literature to find examples of assessments that use one of the following tools:

- electronic portfolios
- computerized grade books that record student performance by objective
- hand-held electronic devices used to record observed student behaviors and skills demonstration
- databases that serve as comprehensive progress reports for parents and the state

I will examine my curriculum to determine where such assessment might prove more effective than objective testing.

2 I will use the chosen assessment during the school year, recording through testing and observation the effectiveness and appropriateness of the methodology.

3 I will report the results of the use of the assessment to the staff development committee and recommend whether the district should encourage its continued use through staff development classes. I will share my findings through in-district workshops or on staff development days.

4 (Optional) I will take a college class, seminar, or workshop on using technology to assist in student assessment.

 ## YOUR PORTFOLIO MIGHT INCLUDE:

1. a variety of quality assessment tools for student projects that require the use of technology

2. an example of a student portfolio and method of evaluating that portfolio in either electronic or print format

3. a computerized tool for collecting data about an entire class with an interpretation of how those data might be interpreted

➤ WHY TEACHERS NEED TECHNOLOGY SKILLS THAT HELP ASSESS STUDENT PERFORMANCE

The too-common practice of granting high school diplomas to students who have not mastered basic reading, writing, and computational skills has led to community demands for more accurate and extensive record keeping. A variety of computerized tools can help teachers meet these demands:

▶ Electronic portfolios are an effective means of storing examples of student work in which specific competencies have been demonstrated. Relatively low-cost mass storage devices—hard drives and tapes with gigabytes of space—are finally making possible this highly desirable but once-impractical means of archiving and retrieving authentic assessments.

▶ Computerized grade books that record student performance by highly specific objectives allow teachers to quickly record mastery of skills by many students and easily report both individual and group achievement. Parents want to see how their child performs compared to the class as a whole.

▶ Hand-held electronic devices can be used to record observed student behaviors and skills demonstration as teachers move about the class. The data contained in them are later downloaded into a grade book or another record-keeping tool on the teacher's desktop computer. This helps eliminate the paper checklists that require extensive data input.

> **Individual student performance data moved to the Internet, accessible by password to ensure privacy, give parents the ability to learn their children's progress throughout the school term.**

▶ Databases that record student performance can be related directly to networked databases of district curriculum, benchmarks, and state standards. Teachers, students, and parents know precisely the expectations of students in every content area at every grade level, *and* how well every student is meeting those expectations.

As the skills and knowledge expected of a student during a grade or class are refined and articulated, this information can be shared with parents to help them become real teaching partners for their children. When teachers can tell in precise and measurable ways what students need to be able to know and do by the end of a unit or course, parents can then provide practice opportunities, check assignments, and monitor progress.

Electronically stored data are more accessible data. Individual student performance data moved to the Internet, accessible by password to ensure privacy, give parents the ability to learn their children's progress throughout the school term. No longer will the conference after six to nine weeks of school be the only means of determining the strengths and weaknesses a student may be developing. This is education in real time.

Knowing a student has received a *B* in English does not tell parents, potential employers, or the students themselves nearly as much as a list of competencies that have been mastered in the course. For already-overburdened teachers, automation of the record-keeping process may be not just an option but an essential survival tool.

VII Individualization of Instruction and Educational Program

SELF-ASSESSMENT

LEVEL 1 I modify my curriculum or instructional methods only for students with identified special needs.

LEVEL 2 I occasionally give students the choice of assignments in my class, but all class members (unless they are in special education) must meet the same learning objectives within the same time frame. Skill remediation is done during summer school or informally during or after school.

LEVEL 3 With the assistance of the student, parents, and appropriate specialists, I create a learning plan for each of my students. I track the accomplishment of learning goals in the plan using a computerized tool. I use this tool during parent conferences and for school or state reporting.

LEVEL 4 I provide suggestions about the content and design of the individualized computerized planning and report tools.

PROFESSIONAL GROWTH PLAN TO MEET THIS COMPETENCY

The growth plan is to be completed with the district assessment director or committee.

1 I will establish a database with a record for each student in my class. This can be a self-designed database, a database template, or commercial database program. Each record will contain fields for:

- learning objectives or levels of performance
- suggested activities and projects that help a student meet those objectives
- multiple methods for determining whether the objectives have been met

2 In conference with parents and any special staff members, I will use the database to help create an individualized instructional plan for the school year for each of my students.

3 This database will be used to record student achievement and serve as the basis for parent-teacher conferences and performance reports, and for any reporting of student achievement required by the school, district, or state.

4 I will work with the appropriate committees to help evaluate and select a common schoolwide version of an individualized instructional plan or modifications to the current version.

5 (Optional) I will train other teachers how to use the database form. I am willing to participate in projects that will make the database accessible to parents through password-protected Internet access. I will take a college class, seminar, or workshop on using technology to assist in developing tools that help produce individualized learning plans.

YOUR PORTFOLIO MIGHT INCLUDE:

1. a database that holds a learning plan for each of a class of students; the database will included personal learning objectives and individualized projects

2. a database of materials and activities that can be sorted by learning style, ability level, and learning objective(s)

WHY TEACHERS NEED TO KNOW HOW TO INDIVIDUALIZE THE EDUCATIONAL PROCESS

One of the most attractive things technology has done lately is what pundits call "mass customization." For most of this century, mass production has allowed the majority of us to own things and purchase services economically; our mass-produced hamburgers, automobiles, and blue jeans are relatively cheap. But the tradeoff has been a lack of choice. Henry Ford summarized the idea nicely saying, "You can have any color car you want so long as it is black." The hand-tailored, the custom-made, and the personalized have been primarily for the wealthy. So too has been "customized" education. Private schools, tutors, and specialized curriculum have not been available for most of us—or for our children.

Our district recently completed its latest strategic plan. One of the strongest recommendations that came from the planning group of parents, teachers, administrators, and community members was that *all* students have an individualized learning plan—in effect, a customized education. There is recognition that every child has special needs and should be expected to perform to a personal high standard rather than a class norm.

How can technology be used to provide a tailor-made experience for every student?

▶ Integrated learning systems already assess, monitor, and give practice in basic skill and content areas to many students. As today's primitive, expensive, and ineffectual products mature, they will begin to take advantage of increased memory, processing speed, and improved artificial intelligences, and quite possibly become Everychild's personal tutor.

▶ Database-managed learning plans may make possible creation of a unique, cooperatively planned course of study for each child. Electronically maintained and analyzed data about a child's interests, abilities, and learning styles could be combined with parental requests and beliefs, and could then be used to suggest content and teaching approaches. Every child would become a "special needs" child because, of course, every child already is.

▶ Distance-learning opportunities, whether delivered on the Internet or through interactive television, will open doors for all students to the finest minds and resources in the world. No longer will students be restricted to learning opportunities that are geographically proximate. Right now students can study with Internet pioneer Adam Engst or graphic designer Robin Williams through DigitalThink **<http://www.digitalthink.com/>**, a collection of commercial online courses, as well as a variety of virtual high schools and colleges throughout the country. Just think of the possibilities for teachers with specialized areas of expertise. Now their knowledge and insights can be shared with students throughout the world.

Parents, who are growing to like their inexpensive blue jeans, hamburgers, computers, and newsfeeds customized by technology, will be expecting increasingly individualized learning opportunities for their children. And teachers will only be able to provide it in an efficient manner if they use technology effectively.

> **Distance-learning opportunities, whether delivered on the Internet or through interactive television, will open doors for all students to the finest minds and resources in the world.**

VIII | Adaptive Technologies

PROFESSIONAL GROWTH PLAN TO MEET THIS COMPETENCY

The growth plan is to be completed with the special education teacher or coordinator.

1 I will determine if any students for whom I have responsibility would benefit from the use of adaptive technologies. These adaptive technologies may include:

- augmentative and alternative communication devices
- switches
- peripherals
- miscellaneous devices
- specialized computer systems
- Braille and other sensory aids

2 I will work with special teachers in the district to determine how adaptive technologies might be best used with my students. I will fully participate in the planning, implementation, and reporting of activities and methods that help students take maximum advantage of adaptive technologies.

3 I will share and use the information I find during inservice workshops, curriculum meetings, and department meetings. I will serve as a resource for other staff members on the use of technology-based educational information and resources.

4 (Optional) I will take a college class, seminar, or workshop on using technology to assist in developing tools that help me locate, assess, and use digital electronic resources.

YOUR PORTFOLIO MIGHT INCLUDE:

1. records of research into the areas of adaptive technologies, including an annotated bibliography of technology-related professional articles, journals, newsletters, and electronic newsletters

2. plans and observations of the use of an adaptive technology used with a student, and written suggestions for other teachers about how to use the technology

3. slideshow and support materials of any professional presentations you have given about the technology

➤ WHY TEACHERS NEED TO KNOW ABOUT ADAPTIVE TECHNOLOGIES

Mainstreaming has placed students with disabilities into the regular classroom. Many of the challenges these students face can be partially overcome through the effective use of technologies, and teachers need to understand how and why special software and hardware is used. A list of adaptive technologies specific to information access and communications includes:

▶ **AUGMENTATIVE AND ALTERNATIVE COMMUNICATION DEVICES.** These include voice-output devices that synthesize speech. Many of these can be programmed with special vocabularies for the individual user.

▶ **SWITCHES.** For students with limited use of their hands and arms, switches controlled by head movements, breath, or other means allow input to computer programs.

▶ **SPECIALIZED COMPUTER SYSTEMS.** Computers that scan and read nearly any text can assist all learners for whom the printed page is not understandable. Keyboards for one-handed typists that use only seven keys and use "chording" as a typing technique are available. Voice input is available for those who cannot type or for whom typing is painful.

▶ **BRAILLE AND SENSORY AIDS.** Braille keyboards, keyboard overlays, and embossers (printers) are all available for both blind students and their teachers.

> Many of the challenges these students face can be partially overcome through the effective use of technologies

FREE ADVICE: The EASI (Equal Access to Software and Information) Internet site **<http://www.isc.rit.edu/~easi/>** is a good source of information related to adaptive technologies.

A list of 10 noteworthy sites that provide information about adaptive technologies can be found in the online publication *Library Hi Tech News* (July–August 1997) at **http://www.net-pubsintl.com/LHTN/pub/134.easi.html.**

▶ **SPECIALIZED SOFTWARE.** Real-time language translators can reduce the frustration of English as a Second Language students and teachers. Spelling and grammar checkers can help special needs students effectively communicate.

▶ **MISCELLANEOUS DEVICES.** Computer programs that read text or numbers, large monitors with large print, and modifications to operating systems to accommodate slower response times can all help students with limited disabilities. Programs like Apple's outSPOKEN give audio cues to onscreen visual images such as icons, windows, menus, and cursor location.

Regardless of the disability, technology can increase the educational opportunities and resources available to all students.

IX | Professional Growth and Communication

SELF-ASSESSMENT

LEVEL 1 I do not use electronic resources for professional growth or communication.

LEVEL 2 I can find lesson plans and some research in online databases. I correspond with parents and other teachers using e-mail.

LEVEL 3 I use the Internet and other online resources to obtain research, teaching materials, and information related to the content of my classes. I read electronic newsletters and journals to keep current on educational practices. I participate in electronic discussion groups and chatrooms that relate to my area of education. I use a computerized presentation program when giving workshops or speaking at conferences. I take part in distance learning opportunities using technology.

LEVEL 4 I organize professional growth opportunities for other teachers and feel comfortable teaching other staff members about the use of technology.

PROFESSIONAL GROWTH PLAN TO MEET THIS COMPETENCY

Growth plan is to be completed with the media specialist or technology coordinator.

1 I will use the Internet and other appropriate technology resources to:

- locate sources of online projects and activities for my students
- locate supplemental content materials for my students
- locate instructional materials such as lesson plans and study guides
- locate current research on educational practices and standards written by professional organizations and governmental agencies
- disseminate information of use to other staff members
- contact other professionals and subject experts
- participate in national or worldwide discussions on educational practice topics
- enhance presentations given to colleagues
- expand my opportunities for learning and professional growth

2 I will develop skills to efficiently and comprehensively search the Internet and articulate criteria for evaluating the accuracy and timeliness of online information. I will know and teach to my students the district's acceptable use policy for network and Internet use.

3 I will share and use the information I find during inservice trainings, workshops, curriculum meetings, and department meetings. I will serve as a resource for other staff members on the use of technology-based educational information and resources.

4 (Optional) I will take a college class, seminar, or workshop on using technology to assist in developing tools that help me locate, assess, and use digital electronic resources.

YOUR PORTFOLIO MIGHT INCLUDE:

1. copies of lesson plans, resource materials, and online interactive projects that have been accessed using the Internet

2. an annotated bibliography of technology-related professional articles, journals, newsletters, and electronic newsletters

3. copies of e-mail or electronic list discussions in which you have participated about educational issues

4. slideshow and support materials of any professional presentations you have given

5. observations and material produced for any online or interactive classes you have taken or taught

➤ WHY TEACHERS NEED TECHNOLOGY SKILLS THAT FACILITATE PROFESSIONAL GROWTH AND COMMUNICATION

There is an old story speculating that if H. G. Wells's time machine had actually been built in the 19th century and used to bring professionals into the last decade of the 20th century, some practitioners would have more difficulty adapting to their new environment than others. Physicians would be lost in a hospital using MRI devices and CAT scans. Bankers would be astounded by electronic fund transfers and ATMs. But many teachers could pick up the same chalk they had left behind in their 19th century schools and continue to lecture as though no time had passed.

Savvy teachers and administrators are accepting that all aspects of the educational process must change to meet the increased demands of an information-based economy. Already home schooling, virtual schools, charter schools, magnet schools, computerized courseware, and a variety of apprentice and school-to-work programs are offering learners incredible educational choices. Our society can no longer afford static, ineffectual schools.

Teachers need resources to help them learn, change, and grow just as much as their students do. Lifelong learning is now a requirement for the adults in our schools as well as the children. Technology can help teachers obtain information, resources, and support for this change process. All teachers need to be able to use the Internet, videoconferencing, and other communication technologies to:

▶ locate sources of online projects and activities

▶ locate supplemental content materials for classroom use

▶ locate tested instructional materials such as lesson plans and study guides

▶ locate current research on educational practices and standards written by post-secondary institutions, professional organizations, and government agencies

▶ disseminate information of use to other staff members in the district and professional colleagues throughout the world

▶ contact other professionals and subject experts

▶ participate in national or worldwide discussions on educational practice topics

▶ enhance presentations given to colleagues

▶ take classes online or over interactive television

On the LM_Net discussion group for school media specialists, Nancy B. Nassar once wrote: "Technology won't replace librarians—librarians who *know* technology will." It's easy to substitute other professions for "librarian" in that statement:

▶ Technology won't replace physicians—physicians who *know* technology will.

▶ Technology won't replace accountants—accountants who *know* technology will.
   Now try these out:

▶ Technology won't replace teachers—teachers who *know* technology will.

▶ Technology won't replace schools—schools that can *effectively* use technology will.

Effective, affordable, universal education has always been a critical component of the American way of life. I predict that technology will be vital in keeping it that way.

X Research and Evaluation of Technology Use

PROFESSIONAL GROWTH PLAN TO MEET THIS COMPETENCY

Growth plan is to be completed with the district assessment director.

1 I will examine my curriculum to determine where I might use technology to improve student learning.

2 I will conduct the lesson, project, or unit and then use one or more of the following tools to determine whether, and how much, the use of technology had an impact on student achievement or classroom climate:

- pre- and post-testing
- comparison of student work from consecutive years
- comparison of student work between control and experimental groups
- records of anecdotal information and observations
- records of classroom behavior, interest, and absenteeism
- student-written comments, surveys, or questionnaires

3 I will look for collaborative data about similar experiments from published research.

4 (Optional) I will participate in university or business studies that try to determine the impact technology has on the learning process. I will take a college class, seminar, or workshop on research methods.

YOUR PORTFOLIO MIGHT INCLUDE:

1. short action research reports of uses you have made of educational technologies

2. conclusions about how technology can be effectively used in the classroom

3. copies of research from professional literature and analyses of how the research can be used to improve instruction

➤ WHY TEACHERS NEED TECHNOLOGY SKILLS THAT FACILITATE RESEARCH AND TECHNOLOGY USE EVALUATION

Schools have been spending a good deal of money on technology over the past few years. One estimate puts the amount at about $4.3 billion for the 1996–97 school year alone, and projections are that $5.2 billion will be spent in 1997–98. Computers, networks, printers, scanners, file servers, CD-ROM drives, and even interactive television facilities are common sights in most schools—perhaps not in the numbers many students, teachers, or parents would like, but certainly in quantities that should suggest this investment is having a major impact on education.

Why then is it difficult, if not impossible, to find definitive studies that show the positive impact computers have had on learning? And why is it vital that we in education begin to find ways to assess that impact?

Let's take the second question first. A backlash against technology has begun in the popular press. Critics rail against technology use for a variety of reasons. A primary concern is that unproven technologies are being purchased at the expense of proven programs, notably the arts. After examining historical uses of technology in the classroom, another analyst predicts that schools will not effectively use computers even when they are present in sufficient numbers. Social commentators have often worried that computers will dehumanize education.

We all know that change always brings the naysayers, both those with political agendas and those with well-meaning educational concerns, out of the woodwork. But even without the detractors, all educators have an ethical responsibility to con-

tinually examine how we use finite funding to make sure we provide the maximum educational bang for the buck.

One reason definitive studies about the effectiveness of technology are not found is that schools do not use information technologies in a single way for a single purpose. Understanding the impact technology is having on education means understanding that there are four major uses of technology in schools and that our approach to evaluating each use needs to be quite different.

USE 1 To improve administrative effectiveness through efficient communication, planning, and record keeping.

USE 2 To provide access to current, accurate, and extensive information resources for all learners in the district and community in a cost-effective and reliable manner.

USE 3 To provide teachers the tools and resources needed to assure that students will meet local and state learning objectives and to have the means to assess and record student progress.

USE 4 To allow students to learn and demonstrate the mastered use of technology to access, process, organize, communicate, and evaluate information in order to answer questions and solve problems.

The public is strongly asking for accountability from its schools and, increasingly, from teachers themselves. Teachers need to be able both to do action research on new educational methods and materials (including those that use technology), and to be able to use technologies to conduct that research. This new and important role will challenge all educators far into the future.

CHAPTER 5

Assessing Staff Development Efforts in Technology

 Happy people evaluate themselves;
unhappy people evaluate others.
—William Glasser

Assessment of staff development efforts needs to be done in the schools on three levels:

▶ personal assessments that are completed by individual teachers and their supervisors or peer review committee

▶ program assessments that are designed to determine the extent to which a single staff development effort has increased teacher technology competence

▶ school or district-wide assessments that are designed to determine the overall level of technology competence of a school staff.

While these three assessments are often done simultaneously and may use the same tools, each needs to be identified and reported out.

▷ PERSONAL ASSESSMENTS

Teachers can easily measure their own technology skills level when given the tools to do so. In fact, it's unfair for a district to demand that a teacher be "computer literate" without being able to describe specifically what it means by the term. Technology skills need to be evaluated with the same emphasis as classroom management skills, content knowledge, and interpersonal skills. Technology skills should be measured on teacher evaluation forms.

▷ METHODS FOR INDIVIDUALS TO DETERMINE TECHNOLOGY SKILL LEVEL

SKILLS RUBRICS

The CODE 77 rubrics, or others like them, can be completed by individuals for their personal use. The rubrics articulate exactly what skills are expected and provide a clear learning path for the learner. These should be self-assessments, but skill attainment can be documented with portfolios of work that demonstrate the skill. (See below.)

A supervisor or staff development committee can, and should, set minimum standards of teacher proficiency if the rubrics are to be used. For example:

▶ A building goal for a year might be that all teachers reach Level 3 (mastery) of basic skills I, II, III, and X during the current school year.

▶ A long-range plan might require that at the end of three years all teachers be at Level 3 of eight of the 10 basic competencies and at least one advanced competency.

▶ Newly hired teachers might be asked to demonstrate Level 3 of six of the 10 basic competencies prior to being considered for employment in the district.

PORTFOLIOS

Participants should keep a portfolio of representative work produced with the computer or accessed using the computer. Participants who are taking the training for college credit, lane advancement, or other compensation like merit pay may be asked to provide portfolio examples correlating with the skill rubrics. Teachers who do not wish to take the classes because of previous skill attainment can demonstrate competency by completing a portfolio.

As with younger students, a major advantage of keeping a portfolio is that it allows the teacher to see growth in skill attainment.

▶ PROGRAM ASSESSMENT

Program assessments need to be designed to evaluate the effectiveness of the skills instruction and the attitude of the participants toward a formal, staff development effort, either by class or by series of classes. Assessments should be completed by at least 90% of participants.

Methods to Determine Program Effectiveness:

SKILLS RUBRICS

Since each rubric describes the abilities required at four skill levels—pre-awareness, awareness, mastery, and expert—participants can do an anonymous self-evaluation of their skills using the rubrics before and after the training program. A comparison of pre- and post-skill levels by participants is made. See the sample below, which shows the improvement made on the word processing rubric after a class and six months' practice time.

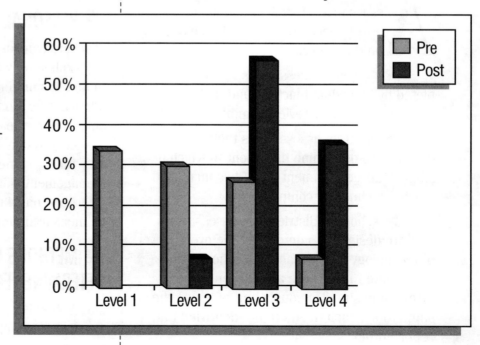

PORTFOLIOS

An overview of all participant portfolios can help determine in what areas a class or program has had an impact. If a high percentage of participants' collected portfolios show examples of e-mail use, the class or program in that area can be considered to be effective.

SURVEY

A survey should be given that asks questions about frequency of hardware and software use and attitudes of the participants toward the program. Participants can reply anonymously. An example of such a survey is in the Appendix as a part of the "End-of-Program Assessment Form."

ANECDOTAL AND INDIRECT INFORMATION

Participants' written comments can be collected and the number of applications to the program for successive years can be compared. These can be grouped by:

- strengths of current program
- suggestions for improvement
- miscellaneous comments

Comments can be generalized. Suggestions made by multiple participants should be noted for special consideration.

SKILL	AVERAGE GAIN	% ACHIEVING MASTERY
I Basic computer operation	1.22	100%
II File management	.99	80%
III. Word processing	1.23	93%
IV. Network use	1.11	33%
V. Graphics use	1.26	53%
VI Student assessment	1.23	82%
VII. Spreadsheet use	1.16	49%
VIII Database use	1.16	51%
IX Hypermedia use	1.03	31%
X. Ethical use	.79	67%

➤ SAMPLE PROGRAM EVALUATION

SKILLS RUBRICS

Analyses of the rubrics have shown that, for all skills, major upward shifts in all levels occurred during the time of the program. For each skill, the first number shows the average level gain made by the group and the second number shows the percentage of participants who achieved master or advanced level.

Nearly all areas show either a high percentage of participants who achieved mastery or an average gain of an entire level.

Some conclusions about computer skill teaching methodology can be drawn:

1 Users need directed learning and hands-on training. Skills that are only demonstrated are not mastered. (The year these data were collected, hypermedia [HyperStudio] and network use were not taught because of a lack of universal accessibility to the program and to the network. Subsequent years have shown growth in these uses comparable to the other computer uses.)

2 Clearly stated objectives, recipe-type handouts, and experienced instructors are essential to skills mastery. A key indicator of a good instructor is one who allows the learner to control the mouse and keyboard while being given individual instruction, rather than taking control him- or herself.

3 Skills need to be set in the larger context of educational use. While all participants receive the same training and show the initial ability to use databases, spreadsheets, and graphics, only the participants who continue to use those applications purposely tend to achieve mastery.

4 The number of skills that participants are asked to master may need to be adjusted.

Ten major skills may be too many to master in the 30 hours of training time available.

5 The skills rubrics themselves are good tools for both evaluation and as guides for the learner. The learner has a gauge and guide during the instruction and for future learning.

PORTFOLIOS

The teacher portfolios showed a wide range of computer applications and productions. These included:

▶ clear and easily modified instructional materials

▶ the teaching of computer productivity skills to students

▶ reviews of educational software

▶ communications with students, parents, the community, other teachers, and administrators

▶ student record keeping, including student portfolios

▶ classroom newspapers

▶ professional newsletters and announcements

▶ online information accessed through a modem

▶ grants, curricula, and continuing education assignments

The submitted portfolios validated the data gathered from the rubrics. Word processing applications were by far the most prevalent samples, but most participants included examples of spreadsheets, databases, and online searches. Many portfolios showed materials produced by applications and programs not taught in class, like programs to create greeting cards, posters, calendars, banners, tests, and crossword puzzles. Most examples showed that teachers were automating current tasks rather than inventing new teaching methodologies or activities.

SURVEY

The equipment and software use survey showed that 97% of the teachers were using their computers daily or regularly. Other applications varied in degree of use. The modem was the least used item, reflecting both the lack of hands-on training for participants in its use and the fact that additional expenses like long distance and online charges would be incurred by participants.

Participants gave a strong positive response to the effect of the computer and training on their teaching. Ninety-five percent of the participants agreed or strongly agreed with the statement, "The availability of a computer has made me a better teacher," and 100% of the participants agreed or strongly agreed that they would recommend the program to other district teachers.

ANECDOTAL AND INDIRECT INFORMATION

The written comments on the evaluation sheets fell into two major categories. Teachers suggested improvements. These included more and continued training, grouping of experienced and inexperienced users, more powerful hardware, and more emphasis on educational software. Participants also praised the program and expressed pride and accomplishment.

Another indirect way of evaluating the program is to compare the number of applications received in each year of the project. For 1995–96, 73 applications were submitted; for 1996–97, 102 applications were submitted; and for 1997–98, 153 teachers indicated they were going to apply for the CODE 77 program. The numbers continued to grow despite a shrinking pool of potential applicants.

▶ INTERPRETATIONS AND OBSERVATIONS
Findings Validate Earlier Studies

Some common observations from professional literature (Apple Classroom of Tomorrow reports) about teachers and computers seem to be validated by the assessments of the CODE 77 project. (Written anecdotal comments from CODE 77 participants are included in italics.)

▶ Teachers with computers expect more from their students, spend more time with individual students, are more comfortable with students working independently or in small groups, and spend less time lecturing and teaching to the whole class.

This computer program has saved me hours of preparation time. ... I have been able to do many things with children and for the children that would not have been possible before.

▶ Teachers are willing to take more risks and see themselves more as coaches and facilitators.

I am no longer intimidated by the computer or by students that have them. I'm not afraid to try different approaches, and very often discover new things.

▶ Collaboration among teachers increases, which results in a more productive work setting. Collaboration includes not just computer skills instruction but course development, classroom procedure development, and administrative tasks.

I have appreciated all the help from former CODE 77 teachers. I am really interested in sharing my knowledge with others

▶ Teachers have a better sense of professional competence as a result of mastering the computer. They believe their students see them as more professional.

Everything I create is so much more professional and takes less time. I keep learning more all the time. Now I feel like a teacher of the '90s.

▶ Team-teaching, interdisciplinary project-based instruction and individualized instruction become more common. Text-based curriculum is first strengthened by the use of technology, then replaced by more dynamic learning experiences.

(Requests for curriculum-specific student software and instruction in using computer-based individualized learning plans and electronic portfolio assessments are common among CODE 77 participants.)

▶ Teachers save significant amounts of time on administrative tasks.

I'm constantly impressed with the speed and professional documents I can now produce. My (students') parents have enjoyed my monthly newsletter. ...

(This program) is the single most valuable thing I have been involved with in 30 years of teaching. And I am just getting started!

▶ It can take four to six years before teachers become comfortable enough with computers to fully integrate them into their classrooms.

I need only time to master those areas of Mac use which remain a blur or even a mystery to me. I am no longer afraid to experiment, but time is on my side. ...I feel great about what (training) I've received so far.

▶ DISTRICT OR BUILDING ASSESSMENTS

Buildings and districts need to determine overall staff levels of technology competence. While this does not need to be done on an annual basis, such assessment should be done as part of formulating a long-range technology plan, staff development plan, or strategic plan. Such studies should also be a part of a whole-school evaluation effort, such as an accreditation study.

Method to determine program effectiveness

The most common and fastest method of establishing baseline data for future planning is a survey. Good surveys have:

▶ a specific set of questions to be answered

▶ descriptive indicators of numerical scales

▶ a rapid means of compiling and reporting data

An example of a professional technology-use survey follows. It should not be used in its entirety but parts of it selected on the basis of the kinds of questions that need to be answered:

▶ What skills do teachers in our district still lack?

▶ Is equipment available in adequate quantities for effective teacher use?

▶ How much is the current equipment being used?

▶ What training opportunities do our teachers like best?

▶ What are our teachers' attitudes toward technology use in the district?

The survey was developed to be accessed online as a networked FileMaker Pro database. A copy of the database can be downloaded from **<http://www.isd77.k12.mn.us/ resources/surveydatabase.html>** at no charge. You must have FileMaker Pro 3.0 or better for either Macintosh or Windows.

> **I am no longer intimidated by the computer or by students that have them.**

Survey of Professional Technology Use, Ability, and Accessibility

The Mankato Survey database was created and tested in February 1997 by the district media staff at Mankato Public Schools, I.S.D. 77, Mankato, Minnesota. The form borrows heavily from a variety of print surveys, and to the authors of those surveys, thank you.

If you have questions or comments or would like the password so you can modify this form, contact Doug Johnson at **djohnsl@mail. isd77.kl2.mn.us** or 507-387-7698. The latest version of this form can be downloaded from **<www.isd77.k12.mn.us/resources/ surveydatabase.html>**.

This template may be freely used and distributed without charge as long as this information screen accompanies it, but may not be sold or repackaged without the author's permission.

While I am happy to answer questions about the survey, I don't provide tech support for FileMaker Pro.

▶ INSTRUCTIONS

A staff member logs on as "staff." He or she is presented with a blank form that can be filled in by clicking on the blank screens and choosing the appropriate response. All forms are either counted or averaged. The "?" is equivalent to a blank box. A final layout that can be printed shows the summaries of all surveys taken. A "find" on any of the top fields will result in a summary by specific type (responses of all elementary teachers or responses of all secretaries).

Some categories have rubrics associated with them. These rubrics are written near the items.

This form works well when shared over a network. Multiple staff members can go to a lab and take the survey at once.

Please answer all the following questions to the best of your ability.

➤ GENERAL INFORMATION

LOCATION_____(name of building)

PRIMARY JOB FUNCTION

Classroom teacher	Media specialist
Special teacher (music, art, pe)	Special education teacher
Guidance counselor/social worker	Office secretary or clerk
Instructional aide	Technical support
Media center or computer support	Custodial/maintenance
Food service	District level administrator/supervisor
Principal/assistant principal	

PRIMARY LEVEL OF INSTRUCTIONAL RESPONSIBILITY

Elementary school   Middle school   High school   District

GENDER

Female   Male

SCHOOL COMPUTER PLATFORM (PRIMARY USE)

Windows   DOS   Apple II   Macintosh   Other   None

HOME COMPUTER PLATFORM (PRIMARY USE)

Windows   DOS   Apple II   Macintosh   Other   None

I HAVE HOME INTERNET ACCESS

Yes   No

▶ APPLICATIONS

Please rate each of the following from 5 (high) to 1 (low) for yourself as a staff member of the school. If you are unsure you may put a ? in the box or leave it blank.

APPLICATIONS	Availability (5-1)	Proficiency (5-1)	Importance (5-1)	Frequency (5-1)
Word processing				
E-mail				
Internet (Web, newsgroups, gophers, Telnet)				
Database				
Spreadsheet				
Research technologies (card catalog, CD-ROM, encyclopedia, magazine indexes)				
Presentation software				
Electronic calendar/scheduler				
Graphics (painting, drawing, PrintShop)				
Assessment (grade books, progress reports, portfolios)				
Multimedia (HyperStudio)				
Instructional software				
Electronic Individualized Education Plans				
Inventory database				
Finance and ordering database				
Curriculum database				
Teacher utilities (test generators, crossword puzzle makers)				
Integration of technology into the curriculum				
Software evaluation				

AVAILABILITY

5 = Available 100% of the time it's needed.
4 = Generally available when needed.
3 = Often delays caused by a shortage at my site.
2 = The building does not have this.
1 = The district does not own this.

PROFICIENCY

5 = I am good enough to teach this to others
4 = I need little additional help or additional training.
3 = I need to improve my skills or learn more features.
2 = I need more training just to learn the basics.
1 = I've never used this.

IMPORTANCE

5 = I would not be able to effectively do my job without this.
4 = This makes my job easier and me much more effective.
3 = On occasion, this is important.
2 = Rarely helpful. I can do my job just fine without it.
1 = This is completely unneeded.

FREQUENCY

5 = at least once a day.
4 = at least once a week.
3 = at least once a month
2 = at least once a year.
1 = very rarely or never..

≥ FREQUENCY OF USE

ITEM (5-1)	
Computer	
CD-ROM drive	
Laserdisc player	
Fax	
Video teleconference	
Voice mail	
Camcorder	
VCR/Cable TV	
Digital camera	
Laser printer	
LCD panel or projector	

FREQUENCY

5 = at least once a day
4 = at least once a week
3 = at least once a month
2 = at least once a year
1 = never

≥ LOCATION

	SCHOOL COMPUTER LAB	CLASSROOM	HOME	OTHER
How frequently do you use a computer in each of these locations? (5-1)				
How frequently do your students use a computer in each of these locations? (5-1)				

≥ ATTITUDES

Using technology makes me more effective.	
Technology helps me organize my work.	
I find the use of technology to be motivating.	
I am comfortable learning about and using technology	
I would like to integrate more technology into my work.	
I would like to integrate more technology into my classroom.	
The building administration encourages the use of technology.	
The district administration encourages the use of technology.	
I feel comfortable helping others in the school with technology.	
I feel comfortable asking others in the school for help with technology.	
I take personal time to learn and practice technology skills.	

3 = Strongly agree
2 = Agree
1 = Disagree
0 = Strongly disagree

▶ INSERVICE TIMES

Please indicate how likely you would be to participate in a technology inservice workshop if offered at these times:

During the school day	
After school	
In the evening	
On the weekend	
During the summer	

3 = Very likely
2 = Likely
1 = Unlikely
0 = Very unlikely

▶ SUPPORT

Please indicate how important the following support is to you:

School-based technology support personnel	
Release time to observe other teachers using technology	
Technology conferences	
Onsite technology workshops	
Classroom computer for teacher use	
Stipend for staff development time	
Computer to take home	
College credit	
Video training tapes	
Staffed technology labs open outside school hours	
Release time for exploring	
Please indicate your level of commitment to technology training over the next year: (3 = Very high, 2 = High, 1 = Low, 0 = Very Low)	

3 = Very important
2 = Important
1 = Unimportant
0 = Would not use

▶ ADDITIONAL WRITTEN COMMENTS

Please add your written comments below.

➤ OBSERVATIONS ABOUT ASSESSMENTS

Findings Give Direction

The results of assessments, especially comments from the participants, help modify the program or district plan to maximize skill achievement and choose skills and materials that are most useful to participants.

Quantitative Analysis Can Be Done on Authentic Assessment

Accurate, measurable growth of skills and attitudes can be shown using authentic assessment techniques. A benchmark for acceptable participant growth can be determined with several years' worth of assessments, and techniques used in training groups that deviate from the benchmark can be analyzed for effective and ineffective instruction.

Long-Term Impact

Over the past years, effective technology training has created a tremendous increase in teacher skills and improvement of attitudes in many districts. Teachers now not only accept the reality of technology in their lives and in the lives of their students, but also actively pursue training and petition for computer equipment. The use of the computer for increased educational effectiveness is now the rule in many districts, not the exception. I believe this step back to teach teachers computer productivity skills will lead to giant strides forward for our students.

Districts that effectively plan and assess teacher technology training have also gained credibility in their communities. While major amounts of time and labor are directed toward staff development activities, too seldom do educators demonstrate the effects of these efforts on school climate, teacher skills or student achievement. The lack of accountability in the use of public funds has eroded the public's faith in education in general, resulting in declining public support. By sharing the quantitative measurements of our staff development programs with the board, parents, and community, we are reversing that trend.

Appendix:
Examples and Handouts

Application Form for CODE 77 Project

The technology budget has funding for the continuation of the CODE 77 project. This year up to 80 classroom and special area teachers will be a part of CODE 77 (Computers On Desks Everywhere in District 77). Our plan is that beginning next fall, *all* teachers will have a networked computer on their desks *and* the skills to use it. In addition, participants who currently have non-networkable computers may trade them in on new machines. If you have a non-networkable computer you want to trade in, you will still need to apply, take five of the 10 training sessions, and give up your old computer and printer. The project has the following guidelines and requirements:

▶ GUIDELINES FOR CODE 77

1 A choice of computer bundles will be given to the individuals who are selected for the CODE 77 project. The bundles for 1996–97 will include either a laptop computer with carrying case or a color desktop computer with a built in CD-ROM drive. Each bundle will also include at minimum a color inkjet printer, Ethernet connector, HyperStudio, and ClarisWorks.

2 These bundles will be assigned to individual classroom teachers, who may use them as long as they remain with the district as full-time professional teaching staff. The computers may be used at home, but must be in classrooms connected to the network while school is in session. The use of these computers by students in the classroom is encouraged. Teaching/learning objectives will be evaluated at the end of the first year by means of skills rubrics, portfolios, and surveys in a report given to the school board.

3 Teachers will be selected for the project on the basis of the current availability they have to a computer. All participants must complete a plan describing their intended uses of the computer. Uses may include, but are not limited to:
- production of teaching materials
- communications with parents and community
- record keeping
- information accessing

- creating and/or using educational programs
- curriculum writing
- software review
- control of audiovisual devices

The proposals will be used to help guide the district's training program. Teachers for whom the PTO or district has already supplied a non-CODE 77 computer in their classroom or office are still eligible for CODE 77.

4 Only individuals, not teams, may apply for the CODE 77 program. A participant may let others use the computer, but only one person will be trained and have responsibility for carrying out the proposal.

▶ PARTICIPANT REQUIREMENTS

1 Participants must be full-time professional teaching staff. The participants will attend 3 half-day computer orientation workshop sessions in June. (An optional special workshop for totally inexperienced computer users will be held prior to regular training.) During this orientation you will be taught the basics of computer set-up, conventions of the operating system, and simple word processing skills. No training time will be reimbursed by the district, since this is a voluntary program. Previous participants need to attend only one summer session.

2 The participants will attend seven additional hands-on workshops in which a variety of computer productivity skills will be taught. These three-hour classes will be held on one of three evenings (to be determined) from mid-September through early November. Previous participants need to attend only four fall sessions.

3 All participants will be required to give a short presentation to the school board at a spring school board meeting about the project, maintain a portfolio of work created, and complete evaluations of the project.

CODE 77 Teacher Proposal

Send in a photocopy this page and keep the original.

NAME _____

TEACHING ASSIGNMENT (grade level or subject and school)

_____

WORK PHONE _____ HOME PHONE _____

CHOOSE ONE.

_____ I have no computer in my classroom or in my office. (HIGHEST PRIORITY)

_____ I have a non-networkable computer in my classroom or in my office.

_____ I have a school-supplied networkable computer in my classroom. (LOWEST PRIORITY)

MY PREFERENCE IS FOR A (circle one):   color desktop with CD-ROM   Laptop

1 If you receive a computer for your professional use, in what way(s) do you intend to use it to increase the opportunities for teaching and learning in your classroom? (Use the back of this sheet.)

2 Is there anything that makes your proposal unique?

3 How will you demonstrate that you have used the computer in the ways you have outlined in #1? (Copies of word-processed documents, summaries of lessons taught, examples of student work, etc.)

If accepted for the project, I agree to fulfill the requirements of the program including attending all training sessions.

SIGNATURE _____ DATE_____

Proposals must be submitted by March 15 to your building principal.
Participants will be notified by April 1.

If you have questions about next year's CODE 77, please call District Media Services. You may send questions about CODE 77 or request an e-mail version of this form by e-mailing **xxx@xxxx.**

Self-Evaluation Rubrics for Basic Teacher Computer Use for CODE 77

Please judge your level of achievement of each of the following competencies. Circle the number that best reflects your current level of skill attainment. (Be honest, but be kind.) At the end of the training program, you will complete the same set of rubrics, which will reflect your level of skill attainment at that time. (Level 3 is considered mastery.) This tool is to help measure the effectiveness of the training program, and to help you to do a self-analysis, determining what areas you should continue to learn and practice. Keep one copy of these rubrics to refer to during the project.

I. BASIC COMPUTER OPERATION

LEVEL 1 I do not use a computer.

LEVEL 2 I can use the computer to run a few specific, preloaded programs. It has little effect on either my work or home life. I am somewhat anxious I might damage the machine or its programs.

LEVEL 3 I can set up my computer and peripheral devices, load software, print, and use most of the operating system tools like the scrapbook, clock, note pad, find command, and trash can (recycling bin). I can format a data disk.

LEVEL 4 I can run two programs simultaneously and have several windows open at the same time. I can customize the look and sounds of my computer. I use techniques like shift-clicking to work with multiple files. I look for programs and techniques to maximize my operating system. I feel confident enough to teach others some basic operations.

II. FILE MANAGEMENT

LEVEL 1 I do not save any documents I create using the computer.

LEVEL 2 I save documents I've created but I cannot choose where they are saved. I do not back up my files.

LEVEL 3 I have a filing system for organizing my files and can locate files quickly and reliably. I back-up my files to floppy disk or other storage device on a regular basis.

LEVEL 4 I regularly run a disk-optimizer on my hard drive and use a back-up program to make copies of my files on a weekly basis. I have a system for archiving files I do not need on a regular basis to conserve my computer's hard drive space.

III. WORD PROCESSING

LEVEL 1 I do not use a word processor, nor can I identify any uses or features it might have which would benefit the way I work.

LEVEL 2 I occasionally use the word processor for simple documents I know I will modify and use again. I generally find it easier to hand write or type most written work I do.

LEVEL 3 I use the word processor for nearly all my written professional work: memos, tests, worksheets, and home communication. I can edit, spell check, and change the format of a document. I can paginate, preview, and print my work. I feel my work looks professional.

LEVEL 4 I use the word processor not only for my work, but have used it with students to help them improve their own communication skills.

IV. NETWORK USE

LEVEL 1 I do not use the online resources available in my building, nor can I identify any uses or features they might have that would benefit the way I work.

LEVEL 2 I understand that there is a large amount of information available to me as a teacher that can be accessed through networks, including the Internet. With the help of the media specialist, I can use the resources on the network in our building.

LEVEL 3 I use the networks to access professional

and personal information from a variety of sources, including networked CD-ROM reference materials, online library catalogs, the ERIC database, and the World Wide Web. I have an e-mail account that I use on a regular basis.

LEVEL 4 Using telecommunications, I am an active participant in online discussions, can download files and programs from remote computers. I use telecommunications with my students.

V   GRAPHICS USE

LEVEL 1 I do not use graphics in my word processing or presentations, nor can I identify any uses or features they might have that would benefit the way I work.

LEVEL 2 I can open and create simple pictures with the painting and drawing programs. I can use programs like PrintShop.

LEVEL 3 I use both premade clip art and simple original graphics in my word processed documents and presentation. I can edit clip art, change its size, and place it on a page. I can purposefully use most of the drawing tools and can group, ungroup, and align objects. I can use the clipboard to take graphics from one application for use in another. The use of graphics in my work helps clarify or amplify my message.

LEVEL 4 I use graphics not only for my work, but have used them with students to help them improve their own communications. I can use graphics and the word processor to create a professional-looking newsletter.

VI.   STUDENT ASSESSMENT

LEVEL 1 I do not use the computer for student assessment.

LEVEL 2 I understand that there are ways I can keep track of student progress using the computer. I keep some student-produced materials on the computer and write evaluations of student work and notes to parents with the word processor.

LEVEL 3 I effectively use an electronic grade book to keep track of student data and/or I keep portfolios of student-produced materials on the computer. I use the electronic data during parent/teacher conferences.

LEVEL 4 I rely on the computer to keep track of outcomes and objectives individual students have mastered. I use that information in determining assignments, teaching strategies, and groupings.

VII.   SPREADSHEET USE

LEVEL 1 I do not use a spreadsheet, nor can I identify any uses or features it might have that would benefit the way I work.

LEVEL 2 I understand the use of a spreadsheet and can navigate within one. I can create a simple spreadsheet that adds a column of numbers.

LEVEL 3 I use a spreadsheet for several applications. These spreadsheets use labels, formulas, and cell references. I can change the format of the spreadsheets by changing column widths and text style. I can use the spreadsheet to make a simple graph or chart.

LEVEL 4 I use the spreadsheet not only for my work, but have used it with students to help them improve their own data keeping and analysis skills.

VIII.   DATABASE USE

LEVEL 1 I do not use a database, nor can I identify any uses or features it might have that would benefit the way I work.

LEVEL 2 I understand the use of a database and can locate information within one that has been premade. I can add or delete data in a database.

LEVEL 3 I use databases for personal applications. I can create an original database—defining fields and creating layouts. I can find, sort, and print information in layouts that are clear and useful to me.

LEVEL 4 I can use formulas with my database to create summaries of numerical data. I can use database information to do mail merge in a word processing document. I use the database not only for my work, but have used it with students to help them improve their own data keeping and analysis skills.

IX HYPERMEDIA USE

LEVEL 1 I do not use hypermedia (HyperStudio), nor can I identify any uses or features it might have that would benefit the way I work.

LEVEL 2 I can navigate through a premade hypermedia program.

LEVEL 3 I can create my own hypermedia stacks for information presentation. These stacks use navigation buttons, sounds, dissolves, graphics, and text fields. I can use an LCD projection device to display the presentation to a class.

LEVEL 4 I use hypermedia with students who are making their own stacks for information keeping and presentation.

X. ETHICAL USE

LEVEL 1 I am not aware of any ethical issues surrounding computer use.

LEVEL 2 I know that some copyright restrictions apply to computer software.

LEVEL 3 I clearly understand the difference between freeware, shareware, and commercial software and the fees involved in the use of each. I know the programs for which the district or my building holds a site license. I understand the school board policy on the use of copyrighted materials. I demonstrate ethical usage of all software and let my students know my personal stand on legal and moral issues involving technology. I know and enforce the school's technology policies and guidelines, including its Internet acceptable use policy. I have a personal philosophy I can articulate regarding the use of technology in education.

LEVEL 4 I am aware of other controversial aspects of technology use including data privacy, equitable access, and free-speech issues. I can speak to a variety of technology issues at my professional association meetings, to parent groups, and to the general community.

CODE 77 Rubrics Assessment Sheet: Pre- and Post-Instruction Self-Evaluation Tool

Please return to instructor after completion. Record your level of attainment of each skill as described by the rubrics as a 1, 2, 3, or 4.

		PRE-INSTRUCTION LEVEL	POST-INSTRUCTION LEVEL
I.	Basic computer operation	_____	_____
II.	File management	_____	_____
III.	Word processing	_____	_____
IV.	Network use	_____	_____
V.	Graphics use	_____	_____
VI.	Student assessment	_____	_____
VII.	Spreadsheet use	_____	_____
VIII.	Database use	_____	_____
IX.	Hypermedia use	_____	_____
X.	Ethical use	_____	_____

NAME: _____

SCHOOL: _____

WORK PHONE: _____

INTERNET E-MAIL ADDRESS: _____

SPECIAL INTERESTS OR NEEDS: _____

End-of-Program Assessment Form

Please complete the following survey for project assessment purposes:

1 I use the following items:

a) Word processor	daily	often	regularly	seldom	never
b) Database	daily	often	regularly	seldom	never
c) Spreadsheet	daily	often	regularly	seldom	never
d) Graphics/clip art	daily	often	regularly	seldom	never
e) Printer	daily	often	regularly	seldom	never
f) E-mail	daily	often	regularly	seldom	never
g) Internet resources	daily	often	regularly	seldom	never
h) Instructional programs	daily	often	regularly	seldom	never
i) Computer grade book	daily	often	regularly	seldom	never
j) Other (list)	daily	often	regularly	seldom	never

2 My students use my CODE 77 computer

daily	often	regularly	seldom	never

3 The availability of a computer has made me a more effective teacher:

strongly agree	agree	no opinion	disagree	strongly disagree

4 I would recommend this program to other I.S.D. 77 teachers:

strongly agree	agree	no opinion	disagree	strongly disagree

5 How can CODE 77 be improved for next year?

6 Comments: (use back if needed)

Sample Skills Tutorial

SENDING AND RECEIVING E-MAIL ATTACHMENTS USING EUDORA LIGHT

by
Sue Krohn
Computer Coordinator
Mankato Area Public Schools

Sending computer files as attachments is a convenient way to share your work with other people or to move a file from your school computer to your home computer. Almost any file can be attached to an e-mail message, including formatted word processing documents, databases, graphics, spreadsheets, fonts, sounds, and even simple programs. This also a good way to send files between two platforms like Macintosh and Windows without worrying about whether the disk drives will work. *Be sure to read the words of caution at the end of this tutorial.*

This tutorial will help you learn how to:
A. configure your computer to receive attachments
B. locate attachments sent to you
C. locate and send attachments to others

A. CONFIGURING YOUR COMPUTER TO RECEIVE ATTACHMENTS

To set a default program with which to open files:

1 Open Eudora. Under the **Special** menu choose **Settings.** Scroll to and highlight the icon labeled **Attachments.**

2 To set your computer to receive attachments as a type of file, like ClarisWorks, click on this button. Locate the word processor with which you wish to open text files.

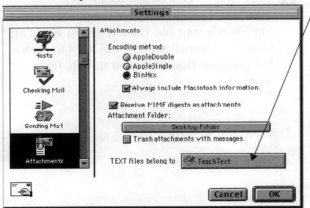

3 Click on the **Open** button.

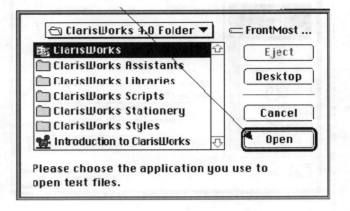

4 Your configuration screen should look like this now.

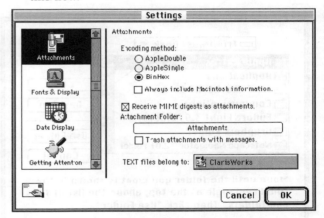

To set a default folder to hold attachments:

5 Before setting the location for the attachments that you receive. I suggest making a folder for them.

To make a folder for attachments:

a) Hide Eudora.

b) Go to the **File** menu and select **New Folder.**

c) Call the untitled folder Attachments. (I like to leave this folder right on my Desktop.)

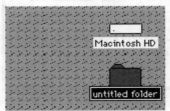

6 Open the Eudora program again. Go to the **Special** menu and select **Settings**. Click in the box under **Attachment Folder:**

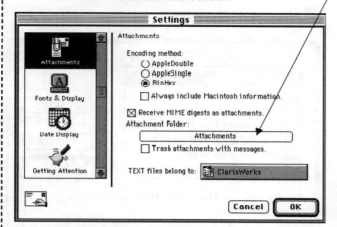

7 Click on the Desktop button.

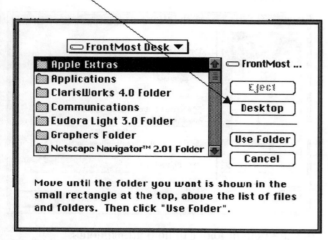

8 When you find your Attachments folder, click on it. Then click on the **Use Folder** button.

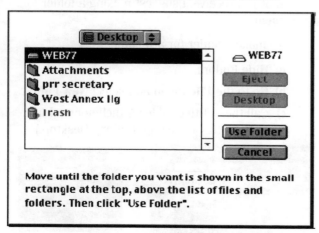

9 When you are back to the Configuration screen, click OK. Attachments that you receive will be found in this folder.

B. LOCATING ATTACHMENTS SENT TO YOUR COMPUTER

1 You will know when there is an attachment sent to you by e-mail. Watch for the small icon that appears next to the sender's name in your In box list.

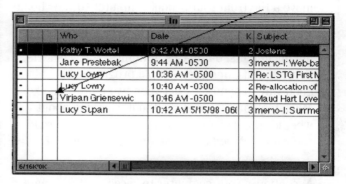

2 In the opened message, you will see an icon with the name of the attached file.

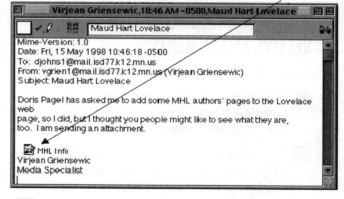

3 Close or hide Eudora and locate your Attachments folder on your computer's desktop. There's your file. Open it as you would any other file. (Sometimes you will need to launch the program first and open the file from within it.)

C. SENDING ATTACHMENTS TO OTHERS

1 Choose **New Message** from the **Message** menu.

2 After completing the text of the message that will accompany the attachment, choose **Attach Document** from the **Message** menu.

3 Locate and select the document you wish to attach. Highlight it and click on **Attach**. This will automatically send the document with the message.

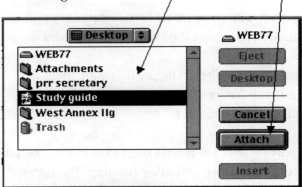

4 The name of your file along with its pathname will appear in the X-Attachments header of your e-mail message.

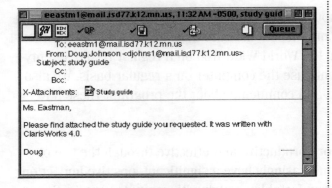

A couple words of caution:

▶ Make sure that the person to whom you are sending an attachment has the same software on his or her machine that you used to create it and the same or more recent version. The body of your e-mail should include information about the software and version that created the attachment. (There are some common file types that can be created with one program and opened with another such as ASCII, RTF, DBF, SYLK, HTML, and GIF. Use them if sending to a wide group of people using various brands of software.

▶ Be careful about using fonts in your documents that don't come installed on all computers. The other person may have the right program, but not the font. Use Times, Courier, or Helvetica, and you should be safe.

▶ Sending very large files may make you unpopular with people who have slow network or dial-in connections. Ask before you send anyone a file over 40K in size.

▶ Never send attachments to an electronic mailing list (listserv).

▶ Some commercial accounts may not allow their users to accept attachments.

When in doubt, ask the recipient to whom you wish to send the file if he or she "does" attachments.

Sample Board Report

April 1

To: School Board and Superintendent
From: District Media Supervisor
Re: Report on CODE 77 project

Dear Sirs and Madams:

The fourth year of the CODE 77 project has just finished. This year 69 district elementary and special education teachers participated in the program. All who began the program completed it.

Find attached an assessment of the skills the participants acquired. The participants spent 30 hours in a laboratory setting. (Thanks to staff and administration of the middle school and high school for the use of their labs two nights a week throughout the fall.)

I have attached a copy of the rubrics by which the participants measured their skill levels. The participants were asked to complete the self-assessment both before and after training. The program goal is to achieve an average gain of one (1.00) level in each skill area, and see a significant percentage of teachers gain mastery. I believe we met that goal in the skill areas to which we devoted class time. (With the availability of the Internet and e-mail, we are actually asking for additional computer skills from teachers.)

We also surveyed the participants about the amount of use that they and their students are giving the computer. It is interesting to note that 91% of teachers indicate that they use e-mail on at least a regular basis, and that 68% of them are using the World Wide Web on a regular basis. Seventy-six percent of teachers indicate that their students use the computer on a regular basis. We also asked teachers for suggestions for improvement and comments about the program. These have been included.

CODE 77 continues to help teachers become more productive and effective through the use of technology. I also believe that the program will increasingly have a significant, positive impact on the teaching process as more teachers become comfortable enough with computer applications to make them a part of an integrated "information skills" strand of their classroom curricula.

The program has been funded again for the next school year.

cc: participants
     principals

Skill Acquisition of This Year's CODE 77 Participants

SKILL	1994-95 (% AT MASTERY, AVERAGE LEVEL GAIN)		1995-96 (% AT MASTERY, AVERAGE LEVEL GAIN)	
1. Basic computer use	100%	1.06	100%	1.20
2. File management	91%	1.02	90%	0.80
3. Word processing	98%	1.12	97%	1.10
4. Spreadsheet	41%	1.10	50%	1.10
5. Database	41%	1.12	37%	0.90
6. Graphics	57%	1.28	63%	1.30
7. HyperMedia	9%	0.42	37%	0.90
8. Network use	33%	1.10	74%	0.90
9. Student assessment	41%	0.97	26%	0.80
10. Ethical use	83%	1.00	87%	0.90

➤ TEACHERS INDICATE THEY USE THE FOLLOWING ITEMS:

Percentages that do not total 100% indicate there were some respondents who did not indicate a level.

a) Word processor	daily 74%	often 24%	regularly 2%	seldom 0%	never 0%
b) Database	daily 2%	often 13%	regularly 30%	seldom 46%	never 9%
c) Spreadsheet	daily 11%	often 16%	regularly 27%	seldom 35%	never 11%
d) Graphics/clip art	daily 11%	often 40%	regularly 22%	seldom 24%	never 3%
e) Printer	daily 76%	often 19%	regularly 2%	seldom 3%	never 0%
f) E-mail	daily 81%	often 5%	regularly 5%	seldom 5%	never 3%
g) Internet (WWW)	daily 27%	often 22%	regularly 19%	seldom 24%	never 8%
h) Instructional programs	daily 15%	often 35%	regularly 20%	seldom 5%	never 25%

2 My students use my CODE 77 computer

daily	often	regularly	seldom	never
49%	16%	11%	16%	5%

3 The availability of a computer has made me a more effective teacher:

strongly agree	agree	no opinion	disagree	strongly disagree
70%	27%	3%	0%	0%

4 I would recommend this program to other I.S.D. 77 teachers:

strongly agree	agree	no opinion	disagree	strongly disagree
96%	4%	0%	0%	0%

5 How can CODE 77 be improved for next year?

- ▶ Needs to be computer class for true beginners. It moved too quickly. Too many people at different levels. (2)
- ▶ Allow computers to be left at home from time to time. Not enough time to work on them in school. (5)
- ▶ More advanced classes
- ▶ Have two sets of classes–beginner and advanced (3)
- ▶ Be sure the computers work all the time and that the printers are hooked up. Have the rooms warmer over the weekend so we could work at school comfortably.
- ▶ Voluntary meetings to talk about what other teachers and buildings are doing.
- ▶ More computers. More programs.
- ▶ Some people my age (64) need more time to grasp these concepts and techniques. My daily prep time is used for preparing my lessons and I'm too tired at 3:30 to deal with the computer. It is also too heavy to haul home for the weekend. The computer is still fascinating to me. I promise to take some classes this summer and practice, practice, practice!!
- ▶ Keep the classes in all areas of the computer. It is difficult to learn it all at once.
- ▶ Make it available to all teachers without a computer.
- ▶ Received information before I was ready for it (e-mail before the building was fully networked.) Appreciated all the handouts. I've made it into a reference book.
- ▶ Group lessons together with more time in between. More time to practice/absorb.
- ▶ Selection process tends to alienate some people. I'm not sure how to do this in a more fair way, but I sense some negative vibes from those not selected.

6 Comments:

- ▶ Wonderful program and instructors (7)
- ▶ Additional computer has made teaching encyclopedia and card catalog much easier. All K-5 students have had numerous experiences with interactive programs.
- ▶ I was very thankful for the opportunity to learn. It pushed me into the world of computers.
- ▶ If all members of a building/department have e-mail, it is an effective method of communicating
- ▶ I don't know how I did it when sharing one computer with 11 people. Having one on my desk, it's used much more.
- ▶ I am proud to be a teacher in District 77. We have come a long way in just a few years.
- ▶ Continue the great inservices and training. (3)
- ▶ I love my LC580!!! So do my students!
- ▶ I have enjoyed the CODE 77 support system very much!
- ▶ I've spent many hours on the computer in the past months. I've learned a lot and continue to grow each day in my computer skills. Using e-mail has increased communication which is so important in my job. (My husband is ready to purchase a computer

for our home so he can get a meal on time!) I'm always at school on the computer. Time just gets away when you're having fun. Thanks to the great media staff that is always available to answer questions and help me out.

► Looking forward to summer academy. Please continue with the evening classes.

► What an essential tool. Thank you!

► I am on the computer at 6:45 am and on usually until 5:00 pm. Can't wait to get hooked up at home this summer. I feel I haven't touched the broad spectrum of computer use – so much available! Looking for a way to make the computer more accessible for my students. I have used it for my classes, i.e., BodyWorks, etc., but not for students individually. Has saved me hours of work at conference time. E-mail has been great.

► Makes my reports look more professional.

► Training is essential. Keep the 30–hour component!

► I've learned a lot – more to learn of course. I've tried really hard to have students use the computer as applied to the curriculum – slow going especially finding time for them to get involved in learning use and completion of projects.

► This program has been very informative and has enabled me to grow more in my teaching than anything I have been involved in 20 years of education. *Muchas gracias* to the instructors and district for their support.

► One computer: 26 students is extremely limiting.

Sample Technology Academy Brochure

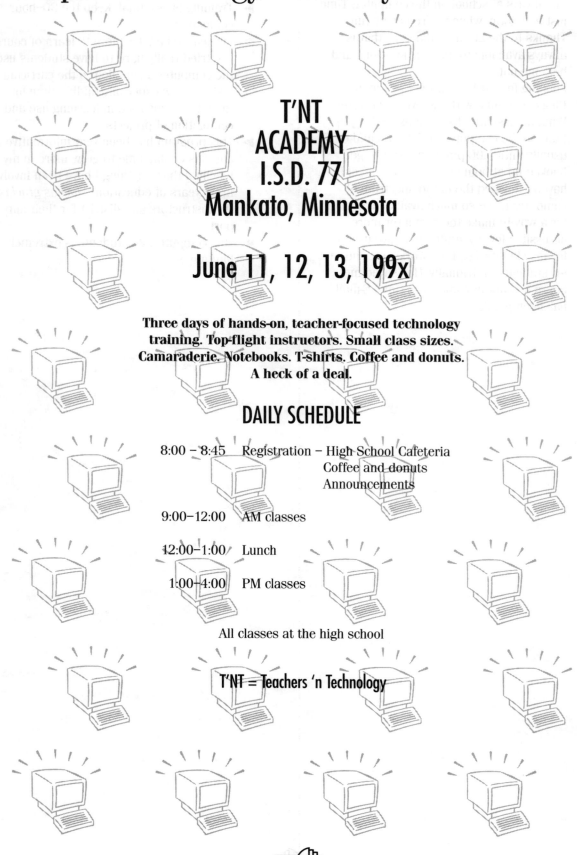

T'NT
ACADEMY
I.S.D. 77
Mankato, Minnesota

June 11, 12, 13, 199x

Three days of hands-on, teacher-focused technology training. Top-flight instructors. Small class sizes. Camaraderie. Notebooks. T-shirts. Coffee and donuts. A heck of a deal.

DAILY SCHEDULE

8:00 – 8:45   Registration – High School Cafeteria
Coffee and donuts
Announcements

9:00–12:00   AM classes

12:00–1:00   Lunch

1:00–4:00   PM classes

All classes at the high school

T'NT = Teachers 'n Technology

1. SCHEDULE

	TUESDAY	WEDNESDAY	THURSDAY
Room 218 – High School	1) Adv Word Processing (AM)	9) Beginning Database (AM)	18) One Computer Classroom (AM)
	2) Quicken (PM)	10) Intermediate Database (PM)	19) KidPix (PM)
Room 220 – High School	3) Slideshow (ALL DAY)	11) Beginning E-Mail (AM)	20) Creating Your Own Web Page (ALL DAY)
		12) Intermediate E-Mail (PM)	
Media Center Lab – High School	4) Using World Wide Web (AM)	13) Shareware from the Internet (AM)	21) Using World Wide Web (AM)
	5) Internet in the Classroom (PM)	14) Using the World Wide Web (PM)	22) WWW in the Classroom (PM)
Media Center Research Stations	6) Spreadsheet Review (AM)	15) CD-ROM for Elem (AM)¹	23) The Writing Center (AM)
	7) Tech: Whole Language (PM)	16) Software for Elem (PM)	24) Charting Your Family Tree (PM)
Tech Ed – High Annex	8) Graphics (ALL DAY)	17) Classroom Newsletter (ALL DAY)	25) HyperStudio (ALL DAY)

CLASS DESCRIPTIONS:

Tuesday

1 Advanced Word Processing, Wortel
Major objectives:
Advanced editing features of ClarisWorks
- Creating stationery files
- Columns/tables
- Graphics
- Outlines
- Footnotes

2 Using Quicken to Keep School Records, Stoffel
Major objectives:
- Learn how to put your staff development records on the computer
- Print a copy of your monthly transactions
- Print a copy of itemized category reports monthly

3 Creating a Slideshow, Jensen and Lutz
Major objectives:
- Tips for effective presentation
- Create slides with ClarisWorks
- Add visual effects
- Set up slides
- Run Slide Show

4 Using the World Wide Web, AM, Green
Major objectives:
- Understand URLs and what you do with them
- Navigate the Internet with Netscape browser
- Select the best tool for a particular task
- Overview of some of the best resource sites

5 Using Internet in the Classroom, Wortel
Major objectives:
- Find locations for students in a classroom setting
- Find locations for personal and professional use
- Access and download sounds, graphics, and programs
- Review of WWW sites for education
- Suggested projects and activities

6 Spreadsheet Review, Bodey
Major objectives:
- Function and uses of the ClarisWorks spreadsheet
- Enter labels, data, and referents
- Use simple formulas
- Create a chart
- Format and print a spreadsheet

7 Technology: Complementing a Whole Language Environment, K-6, Bodey
Major objectives:
- How students can use technology to discover information and communicate ideas
- Examine successful projects

8 Graphics, Krohn
Major objectives:
- Basic tools in ClarisWorks drawing program
- Use handles
- Duplicate, group and align images
- Import clip art
- Paste graphics into a text document

Wednesday

9 Beginning Database, Hanson
Major objectives:
- Understand database terminology in ClarisWorks
- Create fields
- Enter and edit data
- View, find, organize and sort data
- Change the layout and create a columnar report

10 Intermediate Database, Hanson
Major objectives:
- Create six types of data fields and auto-entry
- Create predefined fields
- Enter, edit, view, find, organize, and sort data
- Create a columnar report with a sub-summary and grand summary
- Add a header, footer, and graphics to your report

11 Beginning E-Mail, Jensen and Lutz
Major objectives:
- Understand addresses and configure Eudora
- Send and receive messages
- Reply to messages
- Create signatures and nicknames
- Use proper netiquette

12 Advanced E-Mail, Jensen and Lutz
Major objectives:
- Paste from ClarisWorks into Eudora
- Use newsgroups
- Send, receive and read attachments
- Send mail to commercial newsgroups

13 Shareware from the Internet, Krohn
Major objectives:
- Find , download, extract, and use shareware programs on the Internet
- Understand viruses and virus protection

14 Using the World Wide Web, AM, Green
(Repeat of session 4)
Major objectives:
- Understand URLs and what you do with them
- Navigate the Internet with Netscape browser
- Select the best route for a particular task
- Overview of some of the best resource sites

15 CD-ROM Applications for Elementary Teachers, Stoffel
Major objectives:
- Review a wide range of the newest CD-ROM products for the elementary classroom
- Learn methods for integrating the programs into curriculum
- Hands-on practice with programs

16 Software for Elementary Classrooms, Krohn
Major objectives:
- Become familiar with a variety of software titles
- Understand how computers can be used in the elementary classroom
- Become more familiar with the computer

17 Creating a Classroom Newsletter, Hatleli
Major objectives:
- Create a newsletter in the draw mode of ClarisWorks
- Create text frame links to make columns
- Add graphics to the newsletter
- Extra time for experimentation
- Handout with step by step directions
(Not geared for advanced ClarisWorks users)

Thursday

18 The One-Computer Classroom, Smith
Major objectives:
- Learn ways to make the most of one computer in a classroom
- Based on Tom Snyder's workshop
- Use the computer with small and large groups
- Specific titles demonstrated

19 KidPix in the Classroom, Smith
Major objectives:
- Learn to use a fun paint program just for kids
- Create a slideshow
- Ideas for integrating KidPix into your curriculum

20 Creating a World Wide Web Home Page, Krohn
Major objectives:
- Learn basic HTML format
- Create links to favorite WWW sites
- Use a GIF converter and add GIF files to your page
- Extra time for experimentation
- Handout with step-by-step directions

21 Using the World Wide Web, AM, Green
(Repeat of session 4)
Major objectives:
- Understand URLs and what you do with them
- Navigate the Internet with Netscape browser
- Select the best tool for a particular task
- Overview of some of the best resource sites

22 Using Internet in the Classroom, Wortel
(repeat of session 5)
Major objectives:
- Find locations for students in a classroom setting
- Find locations for personal and professional use
- Access and download sounds, graphics, and programs
- Review WWW sites for education
- Suggested projects and activities

23 Using the Writing Center in the Classroom, Stoffel
Major objectives:
- Teach your students how to use the program for reports
- Create professional-looking newsletters for classroom communication
- Use the many graphics that the program provides

24 Charting Your Family Tree, Green
Major topics:
- Use the Reunion program to chart a family tree
- Create classroom activities using this program

25 HyperStudio in the Classroom, Hatleli
Major objectives:
- Create a multimedia report
- Link pages
- Create buttons and text items
- Import QuickTime movies, scanned images, sound
- Extra time for experimentation
- Handout with step-by-step directions
For beginning HyperStudio users

▶ PARTICIPANT REGISTRATION INFORMATION

No class will have more than 20 participants, and there will be an assistant in each class over 10. Each class has stated learning objectives, and you will have a chance to anonymously evaluate the course and the instructor. Contact your university adviser to see if you can receive independent study credits for participating in classes. Staff development clock hours will be awarded.

All participants registered by May 24 will receive a notebook, pen, and computer disk.

There is a $10 registration fee and a charge of $35 for each half-day class or $70 for each full-day class. You may sign up for as many classes as you wish. All registrations must include a check (no POs) for full payment. Refunds will not be given after May 26, but you may send someone in your place. All classes will be filled on a first-come, first-serve basis.

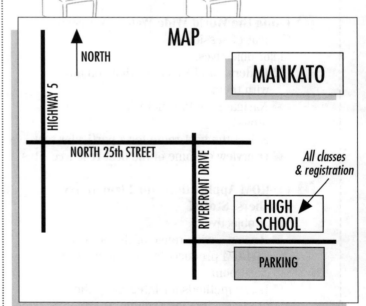

MAP

NORTH

HIGHWAY 5

NORTH 25th STREET

RIVERFRONT DRIVE

MANKATO

All classes & registration

HIGH SCHOOL

PARKING

T'NT Academy Registration Form

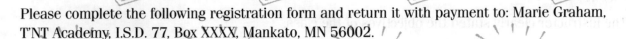

(Send us a photocopy and keep this for your records.)

Please complete the following registration form and return it with payment to: Marie Graham,
T'NT Academy, I.S.D. 77, Box XXXX, Mankato, MN 56002.

Name _____   School _____

Address _____

City and Zip _____

E-Mail _____   Daytime phone _____

Please list the course numbers of the classes you wish to take from the schedule:

TUESDAY	am	_____ 1st choice	_____ 2nd choice
	pm	_____ 1st choice	_____ 2nd choice
WEDNESDAY	am	_____ 1st choice	_____ 2nd choice
	pm	_____ 1st choice	_____ 2nd choice
THURSDAY	am	_____ 1st choice	_____ 2nd choice
	pm	_____ 1st choice	_____ 2nd choice

FEES: Number of half days _____ X $35 = _____

Registration fee $10

Total enclosed   _____

You will be mailed (or e-mailed) a confirmation of registration if this form is received by May 24.

Sample Instructor/Class Evaluation Form

Please take a few moments to fill out the following evaluation of the workshop you have taken. We will use the information when setting up next year's academy.

COURSE TITLE:

Instructor:

1 The instructor clearly stated the objectives of the class.

agree   7   6   5   4   3   2   1   disagree

2 The objectives were appropriate for the amount of time available for instruction.

agree   7   6   5   4   3   2   1   disagree

3 The instructor taught to the objectives.

agree   7   6   5   4   3   2   1   disagree

4 A hands-on rather than lecture method was used for instruction.

agree   7   6   5   4   3   2   1   disagree

5 The instructor was knowledgeable about his or her subject.

agree   7   6   5   4   3   2   1   disagree

6 The rate of instruction was appropriate.

agree   7   6   5   4   3   2   1   disagree

7 The instructor used examples and activities that were meaningful to you as a teacher.

agree   7   6   5   4   3   2   1   disagree

8 The instructor was approachable and used humor when appropriate.

agree   7   6   5   4   3   2   1   disagree

9 This instructor should teach this class next year.

agree   7   6   5   4   3   2   1   disagree

10 I would rate this class as very valuable.

agree   7   6   5   4   3   2   1   disagree

11 How could this class be improved?

12 How could the T'nT workshops be improved?

13 What class offerings or software training would you like to see offered next year?

Sample Personal Internet Term Glossary

INSTRUCTIONS: Record your own definitions for these terms as you complete the program. Add any other terms you would findhelpful to remember.

Adobe Acrobat Reader

ASCII

AUP

Binary files

CGI

Chat/MUD/MOO

Chatroom

Clients and servers

Dial-up connections

Direct network connections

EFF

FAQS

File compression

Frame relay/ISDN

FTP

GIF converters

Helper applications

Hits

HTML

HTTP

Hypertext

Intranet

JPEG

Jughead

Kermit

Link

Glossary continued

Listserv

Mailing list

Modem

Netiquette

Newsreader

Patches

Plug-ins

Push technology

QuickTime

RealAudio

Real-time

Router

Search engine

SLIP/PPP

Sound Machine

Streaming

Stuffit and UnZip

Synchronous/asynchronous communication

Tags

TCP/IP

Telnet

Terminal emulation

URL

Usenet news

Veronica

Virus (computer)

VT100

Wintel

Author Biography

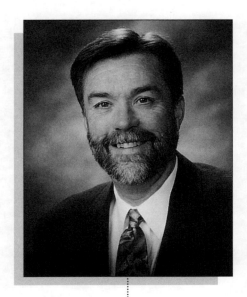

Doug Johnson's professional experience includes teaching junior high and high school English. 13 years of experience as a school media specialist at all grade levels and seven years as a district media supervisor for the Mankato, (Minnesota), schools. Doug also teaches classes on adolescent materials, information and society; educational computing, school library administration, and Internet for school media professionals for Mankato State University as an adjunct faculty member of the Library Media Education department.

His education includes a bachelor's degree in English education from the University of Northern Colorado and a master's degree in library science from the University of Iowa.

Besides Doug's monthly "Head for the Edge" column in **THE BOOK REPORT** and **LIBRARY TALK**, his articles and commentaries have appeared in MultiMedia Schools, School Library Journal, Electronic Learning, Internet Research, The Minneapolis Star Tribune, Minnesota Media and Cricket. He is author of The Indispensable Librarian: Surviving (and Thriving) in School Media Centers in the Information Age. Doug has given workshops, presentations and keynote talks for organizations throughout the United States as well as in Canada, Malaysia, Kenya, and Thailand.

Brown School Media Center
2831 W. Garden Lane
St. Joseph, MI 49085
616-982-4632

DATE DUE

Demco, Inc. 38-293